S0-CFI-767

This fourth book in the Master Thinking Skills series is designed to enhance and improve thinking skills through a variety of thought-provoking exercises that stress comprehension and recall. Students will also learn how to outline, summarize and take notes. More practice is provided in the use of library skills, and students will be taught how to use the encyclopedia. Students will write a report that puts to practical use the research skills they have mastered.

Table of Contents

Glossary

Finding the main idea. Finding the most important points.

Introducing the encyclopedia. Learning to use the encyclopedia and its index to find information that can be used for reports.

Learning library skills. Learning to use the library card catalog and the dewey decimal system.

Outlining. Writing plans that help organize the writer's thoughts in preparation for writing a paper or another report.

Putting It All Together. Using the encyclopedia, the library and the newly-acquired skills of taking notes, outlining and summarizing to write a report.

Recognizing details. Being able to pick out and remember the who, what, when, where, why and how of what is read.

Summarizing. Writing a short paper to give the main points found in a story or an article.

Taking notes. Writing down important information from a story or an article that can be used later when writing a report.

Busy Beavers

Has anyone ever told you that you are as busy as a beaver? If they have, then they mean that you are very busy. Beavers swim easily in streams, picking up rocks and sticks to build their dams. They gnaw at trees with their big front teeth to cut them down. Then they use parts of the trees to build their houses.

Beavers are clever builders. They know exactly what they need to build their beaver dams. They use mud from the stream to make their homes stay together. They use their tails to pat down the mud.

Beavers put a snug room at the top of their dams for their babies. They store their food underwater. Beavers eat the bark from the trees that they cut down!

Directions: Answer these questions about beavers.

1. The main idea is: (circle one)

   Beavers swim easily in streams.

   Beavers are very busy, and they are good builders.

2. What do beavers use for their homes?

_____

3. What parts of their body do beavers use to build their homes?

_____

Name: _____

Bats!

Bats are unusual animals. Even though they fly, they are not birds. A bat's body is covered with fur. Its wings are made of skin. Bats do not have any feathers.

Bats are the only mammals that fly. A mammal is an animal that has hair, and that feeds its babies with its own milk. We are mammals, too. Mother bats have one or two babies each spring. Baby bats hang onto their mothers until they learn to fly by themselves.

Bats can be many different colors. Most are brown, but some are nearly black, orange, gray or, even green.

Even though many people do not like bats, bats don't usually bother people. Only vampire bats, which live in hot jungles, are very dangerous. Bats in the United States help people. Every year they eat billions and billions of harmful insects! Some bats eat fruit or pollen from flowers.

Directions: Answer these questions about bats.

1. The main idea is: (circle one)

   Bats are unusual birds.

   Bats are unusual animals.

2. What covers a bat's body? _____

3. How do bats in the United States help people?

_____

Puzzle

Directions: Read the clues. Find the answers in the story.

Across:
2. Which bats live in hot jungles?
4. What do bats eat?
5. Most bats are what color?

Down:
1. Bats are not _____.
3. What are bats' wings made of?

Name: _____

Blind Bats!

Bats sleep all day because they cannot see well in the bright sunlight. They hang upside down in dark places such as barns, caves or hollow trees. As soon as darkness begins to fall, bats wake up. They fly around easily and quickly at night.

Bats make sounds that help them fly, even though they cannot see well. People cannot hear these sounds. When bats make the sound, it bounces back at them. Bats can tell is something is in their way because there is an echo. Some people say this is like a radar system!

There are many different kinds of bats, but all of them come out only at night. Some of them fly all night, others fly only in the evening or the early morning. Bats likes to eat at night when they wake up from their long naps.

Many bats eat mosquitoes and moths. But there are some other bats that catch fish swimming in water and eat them. Still other kinds of bats eat birds or mice. Some bats that live in very hot areas eat only some parts of flowers.

Bats that live in cold areas of the country sometimes sleep all winter. That means they hibernate. Other bats that live in cold areas fly to warmer places for the winter!

Directions: Answer these questions about bats.

1. Who cannot hear the sounds bats make? _____

2. What makes it hard for a bat to see? _____

3. When do bats sleep? _____

4. Where do bats live that eat only parts of flowers?

_____

5. Why do bats make sounds?

_____

6. How do the sounds help them?

_____

The White House Legend!

Many presidents have lived in the White House in Washington, D.C. Some people say that President Abraham Lincoln still walks there. Even though President Lincoln has been dead for many years, there is still a room there called the Lincoln Bedroom.

Some people say they have seen Lincoln there. Others say they have heard footsteps. One person even said that she saw Lincoln resting on the bed!

But the Lincoln Bedroom is not where President Lincoln slept when he lived at the White House. It is the room where he had meetings with the people who helped him make decisions.

Grace Coolidge was the first person to report seeing Abraham Lincoln. She was the wife of President Calvin Coolidge. Mrs. Coolidge said she saw him looking out the oval window over the main entrance of the White House! Servants at the White House have said that they have seen the him there, too.

Directions: Answer these questions about the White House Legend.

1. The main idea is: (circle one)

    Some people say President Lincoln is in the White House.

    President Lincoln stays in the Lincoln Bedroom.

2. Where do people say they have seen or heard the President Lincoln?

_____

3. What have people said about the President?

_____

4. Where did Mrs. Coolidge say she saw the President?

_____

_____

Robert E. Lee - emancipation honorable man

Mr. Lincoln

Abraham Lincoln was president of the United States from 1861 to 1865. He was president when the war between the North and the South started. That war divided the United States into two parts. It made Abraham Lincoln very sad. It was called the Civil War.

Abraham Lincoln hated to see the country being hurt by war. He did not want people fighting each other and dying. The United States was split because many of the states in the South wanted to have slavery. Abraham Lincoln was against slavery.

He made a famous speech called the Gettysburg Address. Abraham Lincoln wanted to make sure that the United States stayed one country. It made him very unhappy when some of the states in the South wanted to make another country.

Finally, in 1865 the war was over. The South decided to become part of the United States again. Abraham Lincoln was very happy!

Only 11 days after the war was over Lincoln was killed. He was watching a play at a theater in Washington, D.C. when a man named John Wilkes Booth shot him. He died the next morning on April 15, 1865.

Directions: Answer these questions about Abraham Lincoln.

1. Who was president from 1861-1865? _____

2. What happened while Lincoln was president?

_____

3. When was the war over?

_____

4. Where did Lincoln give his famous speech? _____

5. Why was the war over?

_____

6. How long after the war ended was it until Lincoln died? _____

Easter Eggs, An Old Custom

Coloring Easter eggs is a tradition that came from a far away country called Poland and other countries near it. People there made beautiful eggs using dye and paints. Today, in America, many people still color Easter eggs.

The people who started the tradition liked to get rid of the inside of the egg first. To do this, they put a small pinhole in the pointed end of the egg. Then they made a larger pinhole in the other end of the egg. They put the small hole to their mouth and blew out the inside of the egg into a dish.

Today people usually use eggs that have been hard-boiled. To decorate them, they use crayons to draw lines around them. Then they add other designs with Easter egg dye or food coloring.

Directions: Answer these questions about decorating eggs.

1. The main idea is: (circle one)

    Making Easter eggs in Poland is messy.

    People in Poland and other far-away lands started the tradition of making Easter eggs.

2. How do they get rid of the inside of the egg?

_____

_____

3. What is used to decorate Easter eggs today?

_____

_____

Name: _____

Using Chopsticks!

Asian people have eaten their food with chopsticks for many years. Chopsticks are two thin pieces of wood that are almost pointed on one end.

Chopsticks were used in China thousands of years ago. Ivory, gold or silver chopsticks were even used for special occasions. People who used chopsticks to eat with were considered very smart!

Today even American people sometimes like to use chopsticks! But using chopsticks is not easy. Both chopsticks are held in one hand.

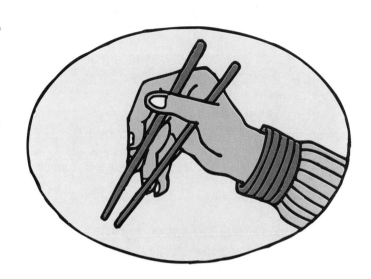

A person holds one chopstick between his thumb and finger. This chopstick is not supposed to move. The other fingers help move the other chopstick. Chopsticks are an old custom with people from Asian countries such as China and Japan. But they use forks and knives, too!

Directions: Answer these questions about chopsticks.

1. Who used chopsticks first? _____

2. What are chopsticks? _____

3. When did the Chinese start using chopsticks?

_____

4. Where are chopsticks also used today?

_____

5. Why is it hard to use chopsticks?

_____

6. How do chopsticks work?

_____

Name: _____

Review

Worry Beads!

Sometimes when Greek people have problems, they work with their worry beads. Worry beads are an old custom from Greece. They help people become calm by counting or moving the beads.

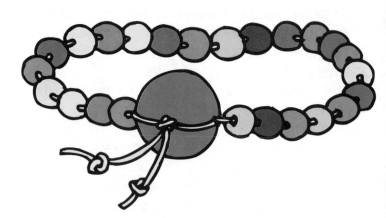

Worry beads look almost like a necklace! They are made out of several beads the size of peas. One big bead can be used, too. The beads are put on a thin piece of leather or a string. Then the string is tied together.

To make worry beads put a knot at one end of the piece of string or leather. Slide the small beads onto the string leaving about an inch of space between the first bead and the knot. Finish the beads with the large bead. Tie a knot around the large bead.

Now if you have a problem, maybe worry beads can help you work it out!

Directions: Answer these questions about Greek tradition.

1. The main idea is: (circle one)

      Worry beads are a Greek custom.

      Worry beads do not look like a necklace.

2. Who uses worry beads? _____

3. What are worry beads?

_____

4. When do people use worry beads? _____

5. Where did that custom come from? _____

6. Why do worry beads help people?

_____

7. How are worry beads used?

_____

A Man Walks on the Moon!

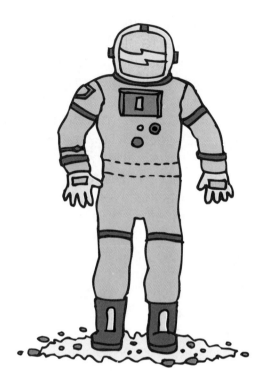

"That's one small step for man, one giant leap for mankind."

That is what Neil Armstrong said when he stepped onto the moon in 1969. Neil Armstrong was the first person to walk on the moon. He was an astronaut who had been in space once before.

This time, though, he went into space with two other astronauts. While one of them circled the moon with part of the spaceship, Armstrong and another astronaut landed on the moon in a special part of the spaceship. That special section was called "Eagle."

Neil Armstrong stepped onto the moon first. While he was doing it, he said the words that are written above. People throughout the world were able to watch on television as Armstrong took his first moon steps!

Armstrong and the other astronaut, Edwin Aldrin, spent more than two hours on the moon. They took pictures. They set up experiments. They even collected rocks!

The two astronauts gathered information that others used in trips to the moon later on.

Directions: Answer these questions about Neil Armstrong.

1. The main idea is: (circle one)

   Neil Armstrong was the first man in outer space.

   Neil Armstrong was the first man to step on the moon.

2. Who went onto the moon with Neil Armstrong?

   _____

3. What did Neil Armstrong say when he stepped on the moon?

   _____

The Moon

The moon floats around the Earth. It is called a satellite. It is very different from the Earth. It has a lot of rocks and dust on it. Craters are big holes on the moon. There are no plants or animals on the moon. Some of the moon's rocks are glassy. They seem to have many different colors in them.

Moon

There is no wind or rain on the moon. The footprints that Neil Armstrong and Edwin Aldrin left on the moon will be there for a long time because the dust does not blow around.

Earth has only one moon. Other planets have more moons. Scientists think that Jupiter has at least 14 moons. Saturn has the largest moon, though. It is called Titan.   People on Earth have been studying the moon for many years. Man-made satellites float around in space taking pictures of the moon. Scientists study the pictures looking for clues about the moon.

Directions: Answer these questions about the moon.

1. The main idea is: (circle one)

    The moon has many rocks.

    The moon circles the Earth, but it is very different from the Earth.

2. What does the moon have on it?

_____

3. What are some moon rocks like?

_____

4. Do planets have only one moon?

_____

Circling the Earth!

John Glenn was the first American to circle the Earth. When someone circles the Earth it is called "orbiting."

It was on February 20, 1962, when John Glenn went into space and started the trip around the Earth. The name of his spaceship was "Friendship 7."

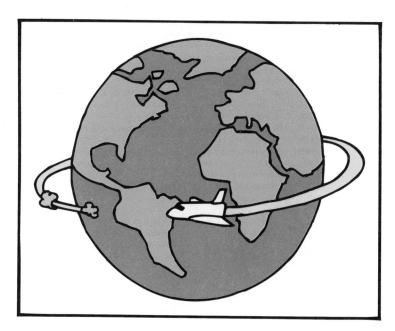

Other American astronauts had already been into space. They knew what it was like to have no gravity. Their work helped John Glenn when he took his flight into space. John Glenn went around the Earth all by himself. He was the only astronaut on board "Friendship 7"!

John Glenn was not the first person to orbit the Earth, though. The year before he went around the Earth, a Russian man did it. Yuri Gagarin was the first person to travel around the Earth.

Directions: Answer these questions about circling the earth.

1. Who was the first American to orbit the Earth? _____

2. What does "orbit" mean?

_____

3. When did John Glenn orbit the Earth? _____

4. Where did John Glenn go to orbit the Earth? _____

5. Why was John Glenn not the first person to ever orbit the Earth?

_____

6. How long was it after the Russian orbited the Earth that John Glenn did it?

_____

Chimponauts Went First!

Chimpanzees went into space before astronauts! In the 1950s, scientists decided to try sending chimps into space because they were much like humans except they were stronger.

The first chimps to ride in a rocket were two named Pat and Mike. Their ride was in 1953. But Ham was the first chimpanzee to go into space. That was in 1961.

Before John Glenn orbited the earth, a chimpanzee had already done it. The chimp, named Enos, had circled the earth twice!

Directions: Answer these questions about Chimponauts.

1. The main idea is: (circle one)

   Chimpanzees are better astronauts.

   Chimpanzees went into space before humans did.

2. Who were the first chimpanzees to ride in a rocket? _____

3. Which chimpanzee orbited the Earth before John Glenn? _____

4. How many times did he circle the Earth? _____

In the word search, find the names of the four chimponauts mentioned in the story.

L	M	P	P	A	T	A
Q	I	O	O	J	O	H
U	K	E	Y	R	E	N
I	E	W	W	P	N	O
O	H	A	M	O	O	T
D	O	D	N	A	S	A

Name: _____

Sally Ride, First Woman in Space

Sally Ride was the first American woman in space. She was only 31 years old when she went into space in 1982. She was also the youngest person ever to go into space!

A lot of people want to be astronauts. When Sally Ride was chosen there were 8,000 people who wanted to be in the class. Only 35 people were picked. Six of those people were women.

Sally Ride rode in the space ship "Challenger." She was called a mission specialist. Like any astronaut, Sally Ride had to study for a couple years before she went into space. She spent six days on her journey. Sally Ride has even written a book for children about her adventure! It is called *To Space and Back.*

Directions: Answer these questions about Sally Ride.

1. Who was the first American woman in space?   _____

2. What was her age?   _____

3. When did she go into space?   _____

4. Where did she stay when she was in space?   _____

5. Why do you think there are so many people who want to be astronauts?

_____

6. How long did Sally Ride have to study to be an astronaut?

_____

Floating in Space!

Life in space is very different than it is on Earth. There is no gravity in space. Gravity is what holds us to the ground. In space, everything floats around.

Astronauts wear suction cups on their shoes to hold them to the floor. At night they do not crawl into bed like you do. Instead, they climb into sleeping bags that hang on the wall and then they zip themselves in. If an astronaut wants a drink of water, he cannot just pour himself a glass. The water would form little balls that would float around the spaceship! Instead, water has to be squirted into the astronauts' mouths from bottles or containers.

When astronauts are in space they do a lot of floating around outside their spaceship. Astronauts always have special jobs to do in space. One astronaut is the pilot of the spaceship. The other astronauts do experiments and gather information about their trip.

Directions: Answer these questions about life in space.

1. The main idea is: (circle one)

    Life in space is much different than it is on Earth.

    Gravity makes life on Earth much different than life in space.

2. What does gravity do?

_____

3. How do astronauts sleep?

_____

4. What do astronauts do in space?

_____

_____

The Future of Space Study

People in charge of the space program in the United States want to keep studying space. They plan to look at the sun and some of the planets in the solar system.

They are interested in exploring Jupiter and all its moons. They also want to look at Venus, which is Earth's neighbor.

Soon they want to build a space station where people can stay while they do some studies. The space station will include places to live, laboratories for experiments, and collectors for solar energy from the sun. People will be able to live in the space station to do long studies and experiments. Scientists say that one day people will be able to live in space all their lives. Some space cities have already been designed!

Directions: Answer these questions about the future of space study.

1. Who wants to keep studying space?

_____

2. What will they study?

_____

3. When will a space station be built? _____

4. Where will people do experiments? _____

5. Why will people need to live at the space station ?

_____

6. How long will people be able to live in space?

_____

Name: _____

Review

Early Ideas about Space

People have dreamed about going into space for hundreds of years. There are legends that tell about inventors who wanted to get birds to fly to the moon. In 1864 a French author named Jules Verne wrote a book called, *From the Earth to the Moon*. In the book he wrote about men being shot into space from a huge gun.

Jules Verne made up that story. Other writers also made up stories about going to the moon. It was during the 1920s that several scientists wrote about sending rockets into space. They decided that liquid fuel was needed. Since then space exploration has come a long way!

A Russian named Aleksei Leonov was the first person in space. An American, Edwin White, went into space next. Both men did experiments that later helped other astronauts in their trips to outer space!

Directions: Answer these questions about the early ideas for space travel.

1. The main idea is: (circle one)

   People have thought about going into space for many years.

   People have thought about going into space since 1920.

2. Who wrote a book called *From the Earth to the Moon*? _____

3. What did he write about?

_____

4. When was that book written?   _____

5. Where was Jules Verne from?   _____

6. Why weren't his ideas used to make a rocket?

_____

7. How did Aleksei Leonov and Edwin White help future astronauts?

_____

Name: _____

Taking Notes

Taking notes is important because it helps you understand what you read or hear. Everyone has his or her own way of taking notes. Here are some things you should remember when taking notes:

✔ Use whole sentences or short phrases.
✔ Make words shorter to save time. For example, "discovery" could become "disc" in your notes.
✔ If you use the same name often in your notes, use initials. For example, George Washington could become G.W.
✔ Be brief, but make sure you can understand your notes.
✔ Number your notes so you can understand where each note starts and stops.

Directions: Do the exercise about taking notes.

Use a piece of paper to cover the story about penguins. Now read the questions. Think about them. Read the story about penguins. Take some notes on another piece of paper that could help you answer the questions.

1. Why are penguins unusual?
2. Do penguins swim?
3. Where do penguins live?
4. Do penguins lay eggs like other birds?

Penguins are Unusual Birds

Penguins may be the most unusual birds. They cannot fly, but they can swim very fast through ice cold water. They can dive deep into the water and they can jump high out of it. Some penguins make their nests out of rocks instead of twigs and grass. Penguins live in very cold parts of the country. Unlike other birds, they only lay one egg at a time.

Right after a mother penguin lays her egg she waddles back to the ocean. The father penguin holds the egg on his feet, covering it with part of his stomach to keep the egg warm. When the egg is ready to hatch, the mother penguin returns. Then the father penguin takes a turn looking for food.

When a penguin swims its white belly and dark back helps it hide from enemies. From in the water, a leopard seal cannot see it. From on top of the water, large birds cannot see it, either. This is how the penguin stays safe! Now complete each sentence about penguins.

Some reasons penguins are unusual birds:

They cannot fly but _____

They can dive deep and _____

Penguins lay only _____

Father penguins keep the egg _____

Mother penguins return when the egg _____

Name: _____

Taking Notes

Directions: Cover the story about raisins with a piece of paper. Look at the questions. Then read the story. Take some notes that help you answer the questions.

1. How do grapes become raisins?
2. How are grapes dried?
3. Why are raisins brown?
4. What makes raisins sweet?

From Grapes to Raisins!

Grapes grow well in places that have a lot of sun. In the United States, California is a big producer of grapes and raisins. When grapes are plump and round, they can be picked from their vines to be made into raisins. After the grapes are picked they are put on big wooden or paper trays. They sit in the sun for many days.

Slowly the grapes begin to dry and turn into wrinkled raisins. The sun causes them to change colors. Grapes turn brown as they become raisins. Machines take the stems off of the raisins. Then the raisins are washed. After being dried again, they are put into boxes.

Some places use machines to make raisins dry faster. The grapes are put into big ovens that have hot air blowing around in them. These ovens make the raisins shrivel and dry.

Raisins are made in many countries that grow grapes. Besides the United States, countries such as Greece, Turkey, Iran, Spain and Australia produce a lot of raisins.

My Notes:

Calif. grows a lot of grapes. After they're picked, they're put on paper or wooden trays to dry. Most have a lot of sun.

_____

_____

_____

_____

_____

_____

Name: _____

Taking Notes

Directions: Cover the story about Graham crackers with a sheet of paper. Look at the questions. Then read the story about Graham crackers. After that, write some notes that could help you answer the questions.

1. Where did Graham crackers come from?
2. Who invented Graham crackers?
3. What are Graham crackers made of?
4. Why were Graham crackers made?

Graham Crackers

Graham crackers were invented around 1830. A minister named Sylvester Graham wanted people to eat healthier foods. He did not think that people should eat meat or white bread. He wanted people to eat more fruits and vegetables and wheat breads that are brown instead of white.

But he had some unusual ideas. He thought people would go crazy if they ate ketchup or mustard. Sylvester Graham was a very unusual man!

Graham crackers were named after him. He liked them because they were made of whole-wheat flour. There are many other kinds of crackers, but not all of them are as good for you as Graham crackers. Graham crackers are still considered a healthy snack!

My Notes:

_____

_____

_____

_____

_____

_____

Name: _____

Taking Notes

Directions: Before you read the story about the history of soccer, ask yourself some questions. For example, "Where is the game from?"

Now read the story. Take some notes that help you answer your questions.

My questions:
1. **Where did the game come from?**

2. _____

3. _____

4. _____

Soccer: An Ancient Game

Soccer is a very old game. It was played thousands of years ago, but the rules varied and everyone played the game differently. By the mid-1800s soccer was a popular sport in England. Everyone still had different rules for the game, however.

In 1863 the Football Association was formed to make standard rules. The Football Association decided that wild kicking was not allowed during the game. The people who liked to kick the ball wildly got together and made their own game. It is called rugby!

Soccer teams have 11 players on them. Only the goalkeeper is allowed to touch the ball with his or her hands. The goalkeeper tries to keep the other team from kicking the ball into the goal.

The rest of the team kicks the ball. The object of the game is for a team to kick the ball into the goal to get points. The team with the most goals at the end of the game wins!

My Notes:

Soccer has been played for 1000s of years.

_____

_____

_____

_____

_____

Name: _____

Taking Notes

Directions: Before you read about the game called cricket, write a few questions that you would ask about it. Then read the story. Take notes to answer those questions.

My questions:

1. **What is cricket?**
2. **When did cricket start?**

3. _____

4. _____

Cricket: English Baseball?

Cricket has been an English sport since at least 1780. Some people say it is like American baseball. There are many differences, however.

In the game of cricket, there is no pitcher. The person who throws the ball is called a "bowler." In cricket there are not four bases. There are only two batsmen who are stationed at something like bases, called wickets.

A wicket is a stump made of three pieces of wood. On top of the stump are two more pieces of wood.

If the bowler knocks off a piece of wood that is on top of the wicket, the batsman is out. If the bowler gets the batsman to hit the ball, other players can try to get him "out".

If the batsman hits the ball, he exchanges places with the batsman on the other wicket. That counts as a run.

My notes:

Cricket came from Eng.

_____

_____

_____

_____

_____

_____

Taking Notes

Directions: This is a story about how skateboards were first made. Before you read the story, write a few questions that you may want to answer. Then read the story. Take a few notes to help you answer those questions.

My questions:

1. **How were skateboards first made?**

2. _____

3. _____

4. _____

From Skates to Boards!

Before the 1960s there were no skateboards. Some people rode on scooters that were bigger than skateboards and had handle bars as well as wheels. But others wanted something more daring, so they invented skateboards in 1963.

The first skateboarders took wheels off of roller skates and attached them to a piece of wood, such as the top of an orange crate. These early skateboards gave a rough ride, though. If the wheel hit something, the board stopped and the rider went flying off.

The first skateboards were manufactured and sold in California. Many people who were surfers started buying the skateboards when there were no waves in the ocean for surfing. The skateboard craze quickly spread and has been popular ever since.

My notes:

Skateboards were invented in the 1960s.

_____

_____

_____

_____

_____

Taking Notes

Directions: Here is a story about the interesting and funny history of roller skating. Write a few questions before you read the story. Read the story and take some notes that will answer your questions.

My questions:

1. **When were roller skates invented?**

2. _____

3. _____

A Humorous Skating Story

People have been roller skating for more than 200 years. The idea to roller skate came from people who liked to ice skate. Ice skating is older than roller skating.

In the beginning, roller skates were made with two or three wheels in a straight line. The wheels were either wooden or rubber.

Funny things happened while people were learning to roller skate. One funny story is about Joseph Merlin. He was a musical instrument maker from a country in Europe called Belgium. He was at a dance in London, skating around with his violin under his chin. The guests at the dance were amazed that this man could play the violin while he was on wheels. The wheels on his skates were put in a straight line, not like the skates you wear today.

But Merlin's skates caused problems! They did not allow him to stop or turn. He crashed into a mirror and injured himself!

Other inventors kept working on roller skates. Finally, in 1863, an American named James L. Plimpton invented a four-wheel skate that became very popular. Early skates had wooden wheels that broke easily. Today skate wheels are made of steel or very heavy plastic. Plimpton opened the first roller skating rink in Rhode Island more than a century ago. People have been skating ever since!

My notes:

Skating for more than 200 yrs.

_____

_____

_____

_____

Review

Directions: Before you read about why people started ice skating, write a few questions that you would like to answer. Then read the story. Take notes to answer your questions.

My Questions:

1. **Why did people start skating?**

2. _____

3. _____

4. _____

Why did People Start Ice Skating?

Ice skating was really a way for people who lived in cold places to get around in the winter. The first ice skaters were from cold countries such as Norway and Sweden. They started ice skating because it helped them get across frozen rivers and lakes easier than walking.

The first ice skates were made from the bones of cows' ribs. The bones were used for the blades, or runners, on the ice skates. People shaped them so they could fasten them on their feet with leather straps.

The first metal blades were much fatter than they are today. The thin metal blades used today on skates allow some skaters to go very fast! New kinds of ice skates let people dance and do figure skating with them. It would be very hard to do figure skating on cow's ribs!

My Notes:

Ice skating helped people get around.

_____

_____

_____

_____

_____

Name: _____

Outlining

Outlines are plans that help you organize your thoughts. If you are writing a paper, an outline helps you decide what to write about. An outline should look similar to this:

An Outline

I. First Main Idea
    A. A smaller idea
        1. An example
        2. An example
II. Second Main Idea
    A. A smaller idea
    B. Another smaller idea
III. Third Main Idea
    A. A smaller idea
    B. Another smaller idea
        1. An example

I. Planting a Garden
    A. Choosing Seeds
        1. Tomatoes
        2. Lettuce
II. Taking Care of the Garden
    A. Pulling the weeds
    B. Watering the garden
III. Picking the Vegetables
    A. Are they ripe?
    B. How to pick them
        1. Pick only the tomato off the vine

Directions: Look at the outline on the right about how to plant a garden. Answer the questions.

1. What are the 3 main ideas here:

1. _____

2. _____

3. _____

2. What are the smaller ideas listed under "Taking Care of the Garden"?

1. _____

2. _____

3. What are the smaller ideas listed under "Picking the Vegetables"?

1. _____

2. _____

4. What is one example listed under the main idea of "Planting a Garden"?

1. _____

Name: _____

Outlining

Directions: Look at the sample outline about building a house. Then follow the instructions to complete your own outline.

I. Finding Some Land
     A. On a hill
     B. By a lake
     C. In the city
II. Gathering Materials
     A. Buying wood
     B. Buying nails
     C. Buying tools
          1. Hammer
          2. Screwdriver
          3. Drill
III. Building the House
     A. Who will use the tools?
     B. Who will carry the wood?

In the city
Buying wood
By a lake
Drill
Who will carry the wood?
Who will use the tools?
On a hill
Buying nails
Buying tools
Screwdriver

Now outline how to build a treehouse. Look at the examples already in the outline. Then choose the other parts of the outline from the choice box. Make sure your outline makes sense!

I. Finding a Tree
     A. **Is it sturdy?**

     B. _____
II. Gathering Supplies

     A. _____

     B. _____
          1. **Hammer**

          2. _____
III. Building the Treehouse

     A. _____

     B. _____

     C. _____

Collecting wood scraps
Is it sturdy?
Hammer
Who will hold the boards?
Who will use the hammer?
Gathering tools
Who will get things off the ground?
Can we climb it easily?
Nails

Name: _____

Outlining

Directions: Make an outline of what you need to do once your tree house is built. Fill in the spaces in the outline with phrases from the choice box.

I. Painting the tree house

    A. **Choosing a color of paint**

    B. _____

        1. **Regular cans of paint**

        2. _____

II. Putting furniture in the tree house

    A. _____

    B. _____

III. Making a visitors policy

    A. _____

        1. **Friends**

        2. _____

        3. _____

    B. _____

Sisters and brothers	Tables
When can they visit?	Regular paint
Parents	Choosing a color of paint
Spray paint	Choosing a kind of paint
Friends	Chairs
	Who can visit?

Name: _____

Christopher Columbus's Voyage

Long ago people in Europe believed the world was flat. They thought that if anyone set sail and did not turn around to come back that they would drop off of the Earth! Christopher Columbus did not believe that. He thought the world was round and he wanted to set sail to prove that. Christopher Columbus wanted the King of Portugal to give him the money for his journey but the king would not. Neither would the kings of England or France. Finally Queen Isabella, of Spain, sent Columbus the money.

With this money Columbus got three ships: the *Pinta*, the *Nina* and the *Santa Maria*. Columbus recruited about 90 sailors from Spain for the voyage in 1492. During their voyage there were many problems with the ships that had to be repaired. Some of the sailors wanted to go back to Spain. They even talked about throwing Columbus overboard and heading home!

Finally Columbus and his sailors spotted land. Columbus thought it was India, but it was really the West Indies, a small group of islands in the Atlantic Ocean. The natives that lived there were friendly. Columbus gave them strings of beads and they gave Columbus and his sailors some tobacco.

Directions: Use phrases from the choice box to complete the outline about Columbus.

I. Christopher Columbus's Ideas

    A. **The world was round**

    B. _____

II. Columbus's Voyage

    A. _____

        1. **Pinta**

        2. _____

        3. _____

    B. **The weather**

    C. _____

III. The New World

    A. _____

    B. _____

The natives
Pinta
His sailors
Nina
The world was round
Three ships
The queen of Spain would
   give him money
Santa Maria
The weather
The land

Sally Ride's Ride

Sally Ride was the first American woman in space. She was one of only six women in her class, and she was only 31 years old. Sally Ride wanted to go into space because she was curious. Before she left for her journey, though, she had to go to school for several months. She also had to do many physical activities that would make her body strong enough to handle the long trip.

When Sally Ride's space rocket took off, she was the only woman aboard. She spent many days doing tests and experiments about outer space with the other astronauts that were on board with her. She also got to see what it was like to live without gravity. She had to eat different food and sleep in a different position. Still, Sally Ride enjoyed her trip into space!

Directions: Use phrases from the choice box to complete the outline about Sally Ride.

I. Sally Ride
    A. **31 years old**

    B. _____

    C. _____

II. Training for Space
    A. **Going to School**

    B. _____

III. Being in Space

    A. _____

    B. _____

        1. **Eating**

        2. _____

> Going to School
> The only woman aboard
> One of six women in her class
> Eating
> Physical activities
> What was having no gravity like?
> Sleeping
> 31 years old
> Why she wanted to be an astronaut

The Mayflower's Voyage

The Mayflower ship left England in 1620. Carrying 101 passengers. Some of those passengers were called pilgrims. Pilgrims are people who had wandered from country to country looking for a place to make their home. It took 66 days to cross the Atlantic. The ship was crowded. There were some accidents on board. The Mayflower landed at the tip of Cape Cod in Massachusetts. Several men searched the area to find the best place to start a colony. They finally settled on Plymouth. The pilgrims lived on the Mayflower through the winter. The Mayflower returned to England in April, 1621. None of the pilgrims went back with it.

Directions: Pretend you must write a paper about the Mayflower, the ship that brought the people to Plymouth Rock. Use the paragraph above to complete the outline of what you would like to write about. Your paper would have to include much more information than the paragraph.

I. The Mayflower Leaves England

     A. _____

     B. _____

         1. _____

         2. _____

II. The Journey

     A. _____

     B. _____

III. Landing in America.

     A. _____

     B. _____

Name: _____

Outlining

The First Thanksgiving

The pilgrims got to Plymouth Rock just as winter set in. Many people died that winter from the cold and from having no food. The following spring, the pilgrims started planting vegetable gardens. An Indian named Squanto helped them. They planted peas, wheat, beans, corn and pumpkins. When fall came, the pilgrims were so glad to have enough food they invited the Indians to share their first Thanksgiving. In addition to things from their garden, they also shared wild geese that they had killed and other food such as sweet potatoes and fresh berries that they had fixed.

Directions: Pretend you must write a paper about the first Thanksgiving dinner. Read the short description above. Then create an outline that you would use to write your paper about the first Thanksgiving. Use winter, spring and fall as your main ideas. Your paper would have to include much more information than the paragraph written above.

I. The First Winter

    A. _____

    B. _____

II. Spring

    A. _____

    B. _____

III. Fall

    A. _____

    B. _____

        1. _____

        2. _____

Review

Pocahontas

Pocahontas was an Indian princess born in 1595, the daughter of the Indian Chief Powhatan. Powhatan had many children, but Pocahontas was said to be his favorite. Her name meant "bright stream between two hills."

When Pocahontas was only 12 years old she met an Englishman named Captain John Smith. Smith had been taken prisoner by some of the Indians. It is said that Pocahontas saved his life when the Indians tried to kill him. Pocahontas liked to hear stories about the English. John Smith made many gifts for her. Many times she tried to make peace between the Indians and the Englishmen. After John Smith went back to England, Pocahontas met and married another Englishman named John Rolfe. Together they had a son. They lived in England for a while, where Pocahontas was treated very well. Just as they were preparing to return to America, Pocahontas became ill. She died of pneumonia in 1617 when she was only 22 years old.

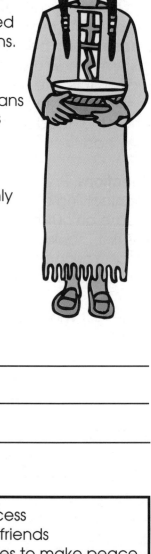

Directions: Pretend that you are writing a paper about Pocahontas, the famous Indian maiden. Read the paragraphs above. Then choose the phrases from the choice box to complete the outline.

I. Pocahontas as a child

     A. _____

        1. _____

     B. _____

II. Pocahontas Meets John Smith

     A. _____

     B. _____

III. Pocahontas Marries John Rolfe

     A. _____

     B. _____

     C. _____

An Indian Princess
They become friends
Pocahontas tries to make peace
"Bright Stream Between Two Hills"
Her father's favorite
She has a son
She lives in England
She dies

Library Skills

Every book in a library is listed in a library catalog. Most library catalogs are drawers full of file cards. Here is an example of a card from a library catalog.

The card catalog helps you find the book you are looking for. Card catalogs list books by their **titles**, their **authors** and their **subjects**. All three of these listings are in ABC order.

```
970.2
G84a        INDIANS
            Gridley, Marion E.
            American Indian Women.
            Hawthorn Books, Inc. 1974
```

For example, if you wanted to find a book titled, *Pocahontas, An Indian Princess*, you would look under P in the card catalog. If you wanted to find other books about Pocahontas, you would also look under P to find others written on that subject. Or, if you knew the name of an author who had written a book about Pocahontas, you could find a card on the book by looking in the card catalog under the author's name.

Many libraries have begun using computers instead of card catalogs. You can use a computer to find books, too. Finding books in a library is not hard if you learn how to use the card catalog!

Directions: Answer the questions about using a card catalog.

1. To find the book *American Indian Women*, would you look under the author card, title card or subject card? _____

2. You would like to find a book about the Cherokee Indians. Which kind of card would you find? _____

3. The book you want to find is called *Animals of Long Ago*. Which kind of card would you find? _____

4. You know that Marion E. Gridley has written books about Indians. You want to read one of her books. Which kind of cards would you use? _____

5. You want to find some books about the moon. Which kind of cards would you use? _____

6. You want to find the book *Easy Microwave Cooking for Kids*. Which card would you find? _____

7. Diana Reische has written a book about the pilgrims. Which kind of card would you find? _____

8. You want help finding out how to use the library. Which kind of cards would you find? _____

9. You want information about the White House where the president lives. Which kind of cards would you find? _____

10. You want to find Claire McInerney's books. Which kind of cards would you find? _____

Name: _____

Library Skills

Directions: Look at the list of authors, subjects and titles. Write **A** for an author, write **S** if it is a subject and write **T** if it is a title. Sort each into the category where it belongs. Alphabetize each category.

(Reminder: Authors are alphabetized with their last name first. Example: Marion E. Gridley is listed as Gridley, Marion E.)

_____ Gallant, Roy A.

_____ Indians

_____ *Animals of Long Ago*

_____ gardens

_____ *The White House*

_____ Sandak, Cass R.

_____ *The Pony Express*

_____ Herbst, Judith

_____ pilgrims

_____ *The Hobbit*

_____ Dicerto, Joseph J.

_____ planets

AUTHOR
Dicerto, Joseph J.

_____

_____

_____

Title

_____

_____

_____

_____

Subject

_____

_____

_____

_____

Name: _____

Library Skills

Look at the three cards from a library card catalog. Each has the same "call number" that shows where to find the book on the library shelves. The other information on the cards is presented differently.

Directions: Answer the questions about what is shown on these cards.

```
970.2
g84A              INDIANS
          Gridley, Marion Eleanor
              American Indian women. Hawthorn Books.
              1974.
A subject card
```

```
970.2
g84A              American Indian women.
          Gridley, Marion Eleanor.
              American Indian women. Hawthorn Books.
              1974.
A title card
```

```
970.2
g84A          Gridley, Marion Eleanor.
              American Indian women.
              Hawthorn Books.  1974
An author card.
```

1. What is at the top of the subject card?

_____

2. What is at the top of the title card?

_____

3. What is at the top of the author card?

_____

4. Why do libraries have three different kinds of cards in the catalog?

_____

5. What is the number listed at the top left of each card?

_____

6. What other information is on the cards?

_____

_____

Name: _____

Library Skills

Directions: Read about the Dewey Decimal System. Then follow the instructions.

Using a card catalog helps you find the book that you want. All nonfiction books — except biographies — are filed according to their number. (Nonfiction books are books based on facts. Biographies are true books that tell about people's lives.)

These numbers are part of the Dewey Decimal System. They are called **call numbers**. Each card in a card catalog will have a book's **call number** on it. Look at the example below.

919.8
B85e   Bringle, Mary.
              Eskimos. F. Watts. 1973

All libraries using the Dewey Decimal System follow the same pattern for filing books. The system divides all nonfiction books into 10 main groups, each represented by numbers.

0-099	General works such as libraries, computers, etc.
100-199	Philosophy
200-299	Religion
300-399	Social Sciences
400-499	Language
500-599	Pure Science such as math, astronomy, chemistry, etc.
600-699	Applied Science such as medicine, engineering, etc.
700-799	Arts and Recreation
800-899	Literature
900-999	History

Each book has a specific call number. For example, a book about ghosts could be 133.1.

Look at where some subjects fall in the Dewey Decimal System.

Pets	630	Maps	910
Baseball	796	Monsters	791
Butterflies	595	Mummies	390
Cooking	640	Presidents	920
Dinosaurs	560	Space	620
Fairy Tales	390	Trees	580

Write the Dewey Decimal Number under which the following books would be found at the library.

_____ *Animals of Long Ago*   _____ *Our American Presidents*
_____ *City Leaves City Trees*   _____ *Mummies Made in Egypt*
_____ *Easy Microwave Cooking for Kids*   _____ *Real-Life Monsters*
_____ *To Space and Back*   _____ *Peter Rabbit*
_____ *Amazing Baseball Teams*   _____ *The Children's Atlas*

Name: _____

Library Skills

Directions: Look at the number on each book. Then use the Dewey Decimal System directory to find out what the book is about. Write the subject of the book on the line.

All libraries that use the Dewey Decimal System follow the same order. For example, all books between 500-599 have to do with science. All books between 900-999 have to do with history. Each library divides its system even further. For example, one library may have kites at 796.15, while another library may have kites at 791.13.

Fossils _____ _____ _____ _____

_____ _____ _____ _____ _____

Dewey Decimal System directory

390-399	Costumes	630-639	Pets
560-569	Fossils	790-795	Magic
580-589	Plants	796-799	Gymnastics
595-599	Big Foot	910-919	Japan
610-619	Human Body	920-929	Presidents

Name: _____

Library Skills

Some books at the library are **not filed** by the Dewey Decimal System. Those books include **biographies** and **most fiction.**

Biographies are books that are written about the lives of people by other people. Many libraries have a special section for biographies. Autobiographies are also included in that section. Autobiographies are books that people write about their own lives.

Fiction books are stories that someone has made up. They are in ABC order and filed by author on the shelves of the fiction section of the library. Nonfiction books are stories that contain facts. Libraries use the Dewey Decimal System to file nonfiction books.

Directions: Look at each book title below. Put a **B** on the line beside it if it is a biography, an **A** if it is an autobiography, an **F** if it is fiction and **NF** if it is nonfiction. Now circle the books that are not filed by the Dewey Decimal System.

___F___ Ramona the Pest

_____ Racing Mini-Cycles

___B___ Abraham Lincoln

___F___ The Jeremy Mouse Book

___A___ Bill Peet: An Autobiography

___F___ Gulliver's Travels

___NF___ From Living Cells to Dinosaurs

___A___ My Life With Chimpanzees

___B___ Michael Jordan, Basketball's Soaring Star

___NF___ The First Book of Presidents

(handwritten notes in right margin: Biography - Tim Haas, Basketball Soaring Star! Mr. Graham, My Life as a Soaring Basketball Star - Tim Haas)

Name: _____

Library Skills

Directions: Now go to the library! Use your new library skills to answer the questions below.

1. Use the card catalog to find a book about dinosaurs. What is its title?

_____

2. Use the card catalog to find the call number for that book. Write the call number down here. _____

3. Who is the author of the book? _____

4. Can you find that book on the shelf? _____

5. Now use the card catalog to find the author of the book, *Mummies Made in Egypt.*
   Aliki

6. Can you use the card catalog to find other books by that author? _____
   List four other books that that author has written.

1. my five senses

2. The gods an goodesses of olympus

3. The story of Johnny Appleseed

4. Manners

7. Use the card catalog to see if your library has a book with "fudge" in its title written by Judy Blume. What is its title?   Fudge-A-mania

8. What is the library's most recent book by Ezra Jack Keats?
   My Dog is Lost, Hi, Cat!, Clementia's Cactus, Apt. 3

41

Name: _____

Review

Directions: Follow the instructions for each set of questions.

1. Write **A**, **S** or **T** beside each line below to say if you would look under author, subject or title in the card catalog at the library.

   _____ dinosaurs
   _____ Russia
   _____ Scarry, Richard
   _____ Christopher, Matt
   _____ Milne, A.A.
   _____ *The Arctic and the Antarctic*
   _____ *The Figure in the Shadows*
   _____ Eskimos

2. Write **True** or **False** beside each sentence.

   _____ A biography is a story that someone writes about him or herself.
   _____ Fiction is a book that uses facts.
   _____ Fiction is a book that some one made up.
   _____ Nonfiction uses facts.
   _____ An autobiography is a story that someone writes about him or herself.
   _____ A biography is the story of someone's life.

3. Look at the library card. Identify the parts that are numbered.

   1
   — 560   2
                            DINOSAURS   ⁄
                         Shapp, Martha and Charles. ⁄ 3
           4 — Animals of long ago.   Franklin Watts. — 6
                  1968. — 5

1. _____

2. _____

3. _____

4. _____

5. _____

6. _____

Name: _____

Introducing Encyclopedia Skills

Encyclopedias are sets of books that give information about different subjects. For example, if you want to know when cars were first made, an encyclopedia could tell you.

Encyclopedias come in sets of 20 or 30 books. They contain a lot of facts. They are called reference books. Each subject listed in them is called an entry.

Some of the best encyclopedias for children are *World Book Encyclopedia*, *Compton's Encyclopedia* or *Children's Britannica*. Some encyclopedias are built around only one subject. The *McGraw-Hill Encyclopedia of Science and Technology* is one of those encyclopedias.

Directions: Information in encyclopedias is in alphabetical order. Brush up on your ABC order by looking at the different subjects that you would find in an encyclopedia. Put them in the right order by writing a number beside each subject.

4	deep-sea diving	9	Little League
5	deer	10	Little Rock
6	Florida	11	meter
12	natural fiber	14	United Nations
3	Death Valley	13	poisin oak
7	flour	1	Air Force
8	Gretzky, Wayne	2	Carter, Jimmy

Name: _____

Introducing Library Skills

Before you to look up something in an encyclopedia, think about the best word to use for it. For example, if you really want to know about ducks, look up the word duck. But if you're interested in knowing something about mallard ducks, then look up mallard ducks in the encyclopedia's index. The index shows the page number and book number, or volume, where the information is located.

Look at the index entry below about Neil Armstrong. Most index entries also tell you when a person lived and died. They will also give you a short description of who the person is.

ARMSTRONG, NEIL   United States astronaut, b. 1930;
was commander of Gemini 8, 1966; was the first man to
walk on the Moon, July 1969.
references in
Astronaut: illus. 2:56
Space travel 17:214b

For example, Neil Armstrong is listed under Astronaut. This entry shows that there is an illustration of Neil Armstrong in 2:56. That means that it is in Volume 2, or the second book in the set of encyclopedias, on page 56. If there is an "a" listed, it means that the article is in the column on the left. If there is a "b" listed, it means it is in the column on the right.

If Neil Armstrong were listed as an article in the encyclopedia, the index would tell you that. It would say something like:

main article Armstrong, Neil
2:87

Directions: Answer the questions about using the encyclopedia's index.

1. According to the index listing for Neil Armstrong, when was he born? _____

   Has he died yet? _____

2. Use the index listing to tell who Neil Armstrong was. _____

3. Use the listing to find out when he walked on the moon. _____

4. Where does this index say you can find information about Neil Armstrong?

_____

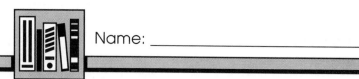

Name: _____

Using The Encyclopedia

Directions: Answser each question about using the encyclopedia.

1. You want to find information about the Tyrannosaurus (Ty-ran-o-sor-us) Rex dinosaur. What would you do first?

_____

2. If there is no listing in the index for Tyrannosaurus, what other subject would you look under?

_____

3. You want to find information about President George Bush. Under which index entry would you look?

_____

4. If there is no separate entry for George Bush, where else could you look?

_____

5. Why should you use the encyclopedia index first?

_____

6. If the encyclopedia says that Tyrannosaurus is in 17:97, what does that mean?

_____

7. If the encyclopedia says "references in," does that refer you to a main article about the subject?

_____

8. Is there always only one place to find a subject in the encyclopedia? Why or why not?

_____

9. Will an encyclopedia index tell you when a person was born? _____

10. You want to find information about the Discovery Spaceship. How would you find it.

_____

_____

Name: _____

Introducing Encyclopedia Skills

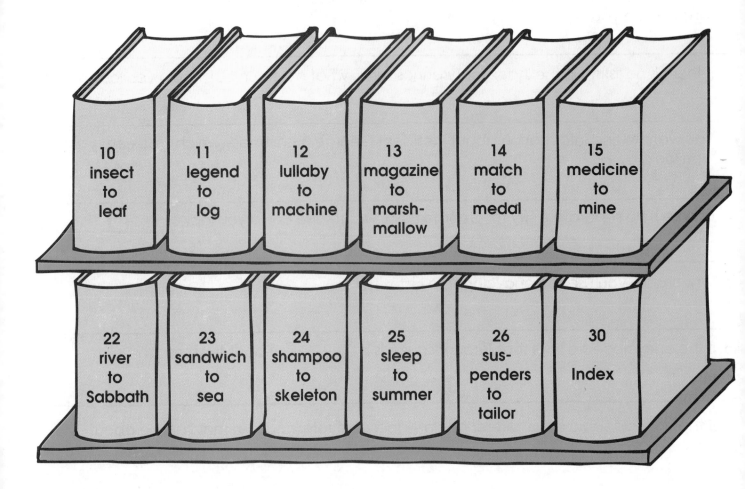

Directions: Look at the row of encyclopedias. Each book has a volume number and the range of subjects that are listed in it. For example, Volume 10 has anything from "insect to leaf." Note that Volume 30 is the Index! Now answer the questions:

_____ 1. Which volume would lung be found in?

_____ 2. Which volume would ladybug be found in?

_____ 3. Which volume would Saturn be found in?

_____ 4. Which volume would swimming be found in?

_____ 5. Which volume would John D. Rockefeller be found in?

_____ 6. Which volume would soccer be found in?

_____ 7. Which volume would magic be found in?

_____ 8. Which volume would melon be found in?

Name: _____

Introducing Encyclopedia Skills

Directions: Find blue jay in the encyclopedia. (Hint: Use the index.) Read the article about blue jays. (It will probably have other information about jays, too.) Take notes. Then answer the questions below.

1. What does the blue jay look like?

   28 - 32 cm long   40 - 45 cm wingspread

2. Name two other kinds of jays.

   Green Jay

3. What do blue jays eat? _They herbivore = plants_
   carnivore = animals

   Blue jays are omniverous.

4. Are blue jays nice birds? _You might be asking yourself,_ _They are_

   No, it is aggressive and it raids the feeder.

5. How do blue jays sound?   _They even_

   They have many different sounds and mimic
   other birds.

6. What do you think blue jays do if they want to eat from a bird feeder where other birds are eating?

   They push all the other birds away.

7. Are all jays blue?   _Irish setter_
                                                       French poodle

   _No_

8. Can blue jays be tamed? _____

Name: _____

Introducing Encyclopedia Skills

Directions: Look up comet in the encyclopedia. Take notes. Then answer the questions.

1. What did the Greeks call comets? _____

2. What does comet mean in Greek? _____

3. Were comets recently discovered? _____

_____

4. What do you have to use sometimes to see comets?

_____

5. Can you ever see comets with your eye?

_____

6. What is the name of the comet that flew close to
   earth in 1986?

_____

7. Who discovered that comet?

_____

8. What did Sir Isaac Newton discover about comets?

_____

9. Are comets lighter or heavier than moons?

_____

10. Does your encyclopedia refer you to other articles that include information about comets?

_____

11. What other articles does your encyclopedia say you should read?

_____

Name: _____

Introducing Encyclopedia Skills

Directions: Read over your notes about comets. Now use your notes to
write a short article describing comets.

_____

_____

_____

_____

_____

_____

_____

_____

_____

_____

_____

_____

_____

_____

Name: _____

Review

Directions: Look at each question about encyclopedias. Follow the instructions.

1. Read each question. Write **True (T)** or **False (F)** on the line beside it.

_____ Every subject you look up in an encyclopedia will have a whole article written about it.

_____ You should always use the index to find a subject in the encyclopedia.

_____ An index may refer you to more than one article about a subject.

_____ Entries in an encyclopedia are in order according to when they happened.

_____ The index will give you some information about your subject.

2. Put the following subjects in ABC order. Write the number of its order on the line beside it.

_____ Bush, George

_____ meteor

_____ planets

_____ Brazil

_____ bush

_____ William I

_____ whole wheat flour

_____ Lincoln, Abraham

_____ Bell, Alexander Graham

_____ Japan

3. Name two places where you could look to find Jupiter in an encyclopedia.

_____

4. Name two possible entries for George Washingon in an encyclopedia.

_____

5. Name one entry that would include information about ants, flies, spiders and gnats.

_____

Summarizing

A summary is a short article that includes only the main points of a longer article, speech or description. For example, a summary of your life would tell when you were born, who your parents are, how many children are in your family, your age and your grade in school. A summary would not tell about your favorite joke or how much homework you had yesterday. Instead, the summary of your life would mention only the basic facts.

Directions: Use the space below to write a summary of your life. Use the information above to help you.

_____

_____

_____

_____

_____

_____

_____

_____

_____

_____

_____

The Cold North Pole

At the North Pole the sun does not shine for half of the year. It stays dark outside. But for the other six months of the year the sun does not set. It is light through the night.

The North Pole is as far north as you can go. If you traveled north to the North Pole and kept going, you would start going south. You could call the North Pole the top of the earth.

The average temperature at the north pole is -9 degrees Fahrenheit. That is not much colder than a lot of towns in the United States get in the winter. In fact, some towns get colder than that. But at the North Pole it stays very cold for a very long time.

With the sun out for 24 hours, the North Pole can get as warm as 38 degrees Fahrenheit in the summer. But that is not quite warm enough to swim, is it?

The cold winds that blow off of the Arctic Ocean make the North Pole a very cold place. The summer temperature only gets to 38 degrees in places that are sheltered from the wind.

The Arctic Ocean is at the North Pole. The area surrounding the North Pole is called the Arctic Region. Some of Canada, Alaska, Greenland, Russia and Scandinavia (Skan-di-na-via) are in the Arctic Region. These places get very cold in the long, dark winters, too!

The main points of this story include:1. The sun is never out in the winter. It is always out in the summer. 2. The North Pole is very cold all year. 3. Winds from the Arctic Ocean make the North Pole stay very cold. The Arctic Ocean surrounds the North Pole. 4. There is some land in the Arctic Region.

Directions: Write a paragraph that summarizes conditions at the North Pole. Use another sheet of paper if necessary.

_____

_____

_____

_____

_____

Name: _____

Eskimos: Great Hunters and Fishermen

Eskimos are hunters and fishermen. There are several different kinds of Eskimos in Russia, Alaska, Canada, Greenland and Scandinavia. For many centuries, Eskimos have been good hunters and fishermen.

The North Alaskan Eskimos are known for hunting the large bowhead whale. The bowhead whale can weigh as much as 60 tons! Eskimos in Greenland fish for cod. Eskimos also fish for the smaller white whale. They also like to catch seals and walruses.

During the short summers in the Arctic, instead of fishing, some Eskimos hunt for animals such as birds and caribou (care-uh-boo). Eskimos in some countries follow herds of reindeer. They use the reindeer for food and transportation. They use its fur and skin for clothing or to trade for other supplies.

Because it is dark in the Arctic Circle for six months of the year, Eskimos do not have a regular time for sleeping. They sleep only when they get tired!

Directions: Think about the main points in the story. Write a summary of **Eskimos: Great Hunters and Fishermen.**

Think about these main points:
1. Eskimos are great hunters and fishermen.
2. Eskimos fish for different things depending on where they live.
3. They hunt for different things depending on where they live.
4. Eskimos do not have a regular time for sleeping because it is dark six months of the year.

_____

_____

_____

_____

_____

_____

Settler Children Were Very Busy

In the 1700s and 1800s many children came to America from other countries. In the beginning, they had no time to go to school. They had to help their families work in the fields, care for the animals and clean the house. They also helped care for their younger brothers and sisters.

Sometimes settler children helped build houses and schools. Usually these early school buildings were just one room. There was only one teacher for all the children. Settler children were very happy when they could attend school.

Because settler children worked so much, they had little time to play. There were not many things settler children could do just for fun. One pastime was gardening. Weeding their gardens taught them how to be orderly. Children sometimes made gifts out of the things they grew.

The settlers also encouraged their children to sing. Each one was expected to play at least one musical instrument. Parents wanted their settler children to walk, ride horses, visit friends and relatives and read nonfiction books.

Most settler children did not have many toys. The toys they owned were made by their parents and grandparents. They were made of cloth or carved from wood. The children made up games out of string, such as "cat's cradle." They also made things out of wood, such as see-saws. Settler children did not have all the toys we have today, but they managed to have fun anyway!

Directions: What are the main points about the first children who came to the United States? Write a summary about settler children.

Here are two main points of the story. Can you name any others?

1. Settler children worked hard.

2. Settler children had many jobs.

3. _____

4. _____

5. _____

Summary:

_____

_____

Name: _____

Putting It All Together

Directions: In this section you will use all of your new skills! Choose a planet in the solar system besides Earth. It can be Mercury, Venus, Mars, Saturn, Jupiter, Uranus, Neptune or Pluto. Answer the following questions about the paper you will write.

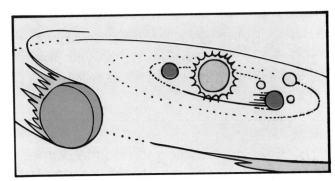

1. What planet are you going to write about?

_____

2. How will you find information about the planet?

_____

3. While you are reading the information, you should **take notes** or **make an outline**. (Circle one.)

4. After you have taken notes about your planet, what should you do next?

_____

5. Can you begin writing your paper after you have made an outline?

_____

6. Think about some of the main points you want to find out about your planet. What are they?

1. _____

2. _____

3. _____

4. _____

5. _____

Name: _____

Putting It All Together

Directions: Look at each question about your planet. Follow the instructions.

1. To begin gathering information about your planet you should look for books about it. Besides books with the planet's name in the title, what other books may have facts about the planet?

_____

2. Use the card catalog to find the names of four books that have information about your planet in them. List their titles, their authors and their call numbers.

TITLE   **AUTHOR**   **CALL NUMBER**

1. **The Golden Book of Stars and Planets, Judith Herbst**

2. _____

3. _____

4. _____

5. _____

3. Name at least two books that you will use for your report.

1. _____

2. _____

4. Begin taking some notes from the books that you have read. Your notes should cover the main points of the stories. Use separate sheets of paper to finish writing your notes.

_____

_____

_____

_____

Name: _____

Putting It All Together

Directions: Now use your encyclopedia skills to get information about your planet. Look at each question. Follow the directions.

1. When you use an encyclopedia to get information, what should you do first?

_____

2. Where does the index say to look for information about your planet?

_____

3. Now write some notes about your planet from the article or articles in the encyclopedia.

_____

_____

_____

_____

_____

_____

_____

_____

Name: _____

Putting It All Together

Directions: It is time to make an outline for your paper about the planet. Look at the outline below. Some of the main points have already been filled in. Complete your outline using the information you have found in books and the encyclopedia.

I. The location of the planet

    A. _____

        1. _____

        2. _____

    B. _____

II. What does the planet look like?

    A. _____

    B. _____

III. What is on the planet?

    A. _____

    B. _____

    C. _____

IV. Could we live here? Why or why not?

    A. _____

    B. _____

    C. _____

Putting It All Together

Directions: Now use your outline and your notes to begin writing a paper about the planet. Use your own paper to finish this writing project.

_____

_____

_____

_____

_____

_____

_____

_____

_____

_____

_____

_____

_____

_____

Review

Directions: Read each question. Follow the instructions.

1. Write **True** or **False** beside each statement.

_____ Card catalogs have four different files.
_____ You can find a book if all you know is the author's name.
_____ Call numbers are listed in the card catalog.
_____ All books in a library are filed by their call numbers.
_____ Biographies have their own section in some libraries.
_____ When you take notes you must write in complete sentences.
_____ Never abbreviate when you take notes.
_____ You should write down a lot when you take notes.
_____ Before you take notes, you should ask yourself what you would like to know.

2. Write the form for an outline.

I. Main Idea

    A. A smaller idea

    B. _____

        1. _____

        2. _____

II. _____

    A. _____

    B. _____

        1. _____

III. _____

3. What do you do when you summarize a story?

_____

_____

Haunted House

This is a map of a haunted house.

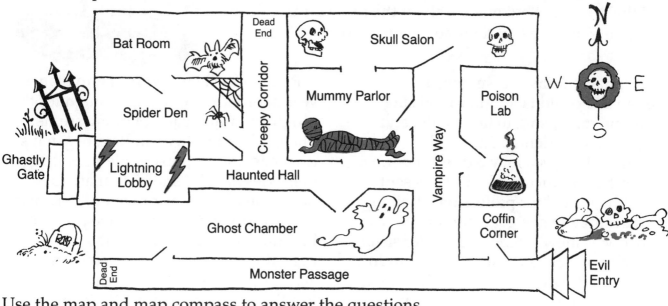

Use the map and map compass to answer the questions.

1. If you are brave enough to enter the house through the Ghastly Gate, what is the first room you come to? _____

2. You walk along the Haunted Hall and then along the Creepy Corridor. What is at the end of the Creepy Corridor? _____

3. You hear strange noises coming from the Bat Room. You want to investigate. Which room do you have to go through to get to the Bat Room? _____

4. You are chased into the Ghost Chamber through the double doors. You escape out the small door to the Monster Passage. If you want to hide in the Coffin Corner, in which direction should you run? _____

5. You have just left the Poison Lab after checking out the equipment. In which direction do you go on Vampire Way to get to the Skull Salon? _____

6. From the Skull Salon you can walk directly into which room? _____

7. After seeing all those mummies in the Mummy Parlor, you have had enough of this haunted house. You go out the door on Vampire Way and run south to the Monster Passage. Then you go east. Through what do you escape? _____

Cross Out

Read each paragraph.
All the sentences but one are about the same idea.
Find the sentence that does not belong and cross it out.

Stephanie Mills was singing almost before she could talk. She would sing with the radio, sing to her family, and sing with her friends. She liked to imagine she was a movie director or an orchestra conductor. Her parents sent her to acting school for professional training, and eventually she got a part in a Broadway show. Stephanie's older sister was also an actress. But Stephanie didn't become a Broadway star until she was 13 and she won the part of Dorothy in a show called *The Wiz*. She played the part for four years, and it was the beginning of her career as a famous singer.

Reid Rondell trained for more than a year in order to be strong enough for the rough and tumble job of doing stunts. Then, when he was ten, Reid began his career as a stunt person. He does things in movies and TV shows that are too dangerous for the actors to do. Reid also likes to surf and water ski. He practices his stunts over and over so that everything is planned out before the stunt is performed. On screen, it looks like the actors are falling off horses, crashing cars, or jumping off mountains. But in reality, stunt people like Reid are doing these things.

One day in 1956, twelve-year-old Bobby Fischer visited the Manhattan Chess Club. He had never played there before, but he felt sure he could beat even the best players in the room. Once Bobby played on a park bench through a rainstorm. Bobby started to play, and a few people came over to watch. Then more people crowded around to watch Bobby make his moves. These men and women were experienced players, yet they were amazed at how brilliantly Bobby played. Little did they know that two years later Bobby would be the chess champion of the United States.

Betty Bennett was just ten years old when she made her first solo airplane flight. Her father sold airplanes and there was an airfield behind her house. She sat in the plane by herself and waited for the engine to warm up. Then she gave the engine more gas, and the plane began to roll forward. It moved slowly at first. Then it raced faster down the runway. Finally the plane lifted into the air like a bird, gliding up into the sky. Betty swooped through the air over blue water. She circled over green fields and forests. When it was time to return, she drifted to the ground in a perfect landing.

What do all the paragraphs above tell about? _____

_____

Identifying the main idea

Ghost Town

Some modern-day explorers discovered a western ghost town.
They made this chart to show what they discovered.

Place Discovered	Dates Explored	Objects Found	Information About Citizens
General Store	September 10–12	herb jars flour sack	Owned by Mr. and Mrs. Bridges
Gold Mine	October 14–17	gold flakes panning equipment mining tools	Operated by G. Lawrence
Jail	October 11–13	sheriff's badge handcuffs	Outlaws killed Sheriff Marks in 1831
Schoolhouse	September 7–8	slate readers	Miss Hastings taught for 25 years

Use the chart to answer the following questions.

1. Which place was explored first? _____

2. Who owned the general store? _____

3. Which places were explored in October? _____

4. What objects were found in the general store? _____

5. Who killed Sheriff Marks? _____

6. In which place were the most objects found? _____

7. Which citizen helped children learn to read? _____

What do you think was the purpose of the exploration?

_____

_____

Locating and using details

All About Me

Ask a family member to help you with these activities.

My Numbers
You can describe yourself with numbers.
Choose eight of the items listed below.
Fill in the circle in front of each item you choose.
Then have your family member help you find the numbers.
Write each number after the item.

○ length of nose _____   ○ number of T-shirts _____

○ length of thumb _____   ○ number of pairs of sneakers _____

○ length of little toe _____   ○ how long it takes to count to 100 _____

○ length of hair _____   ○ how long can hold breath _____

○ length of foot _____   ○ how long it takes to brush teeth _____

○ time born _____   ○ how long it takes to say alphabet _____

○ lucky number _____   ○ how far can jump _____

Rectangle or Square?
You can also describe yourself as a shape.
Get a ball of string and a pair of scissors.
Have your family member cut a piece of string equal
to your height.
Then cut a piece as long as your outstretched arms.
Compare the pieces of string.
If one is longer than the other, you are a rectangle.
If they are the same length, you are a square.
Write your name in the rectangle or square to show
which shape you are.

Consider the new things you learned about yourself.
Which three things were most surprising?

Rectangle

Square

_____   _____   _____

If your friends or other family members are interested, help
them find out their numbers and shapes.

Headlines

Read each newspaper headline.
Circle the statement that gives the probable reason for the headline.

· The Record ·
☆ EXTRA ☆

GIANT WAVES STRIKE COAST

earthquake in Colorado

tornado across Kansas

hurricane near Florida

· The NEWS ·

Famous Actress Gone!

movie star changed name

new movie closed

movie star disappeared

THE GAZETTE

**TONS OF SNOW
ALL ROADS CLOSED**

snow shovelers strike

sudden winter storm

new highway construction

~ The Advance ~

New Crater Discovered on Moon

scientists using powerful new telescopes

astronauts training for space mission

pilots flying world's fastest airplane

Write a reason for this headline on the newspaper.

The Sun

Dallas Knee-Deep in Sheep

explosion in sweater factory

escaped farm animals

people wearing shorts

Our Town News

"Noise Must Stop!" says Mayor

Determining causes of events

Who Did It?

Someone has robbed a bank.
Can you figure out who did it?
The signs the people are holding will give you clues.
After you read each clue, write the first letter of the clue on
the line at the bottom of the page.
Then do what the clue says.
Start by looking for the person who is not afraid of wild animals.

OUT OF LUCK. I DON'T HAVE TIME TO ROB BANKS. LOOK FOR THE PERSON WHO SAYS BALL GAMES ARE THE BEST SHOWS ON TV.

WHAT? I'M NOT THE PERSON YOU WANT. WHY DON'T YOU LOOK FOR THE PERSON WHO THINKS SUPERMARKETS ARE INTERESTING PLACES TO VISIT?

BANKS? I NEVER ROB THEM! TRY LOOKING FOR THE PERSON WHO SPENDS LOTS OF MONEY IN PAINT STORES.

WHY ASK ME? I'M NOT GUILTY. LOOK FOR THE PERSON WHO FEELS AT HOME ON THE RANGE.

YOU SOLVED THE CRIME! JUST READ THE SENTENCE AT THE BOTTOM OF THE PAGE TO FIND OUT WHO ROBBED THE BANK.

I DON'T WANT TO TALK ABOUT IT! LOOK FOR THE PERSON WHO IS ALWAYS TALKING ABOUT VEGETABLES.

OH, NO! I DIDN'T DO IT. YOU SHOULD LOOK FOR THE PERSON WHO IS REALLY GOOD AT SOLVING CRIMES.

COMPLETELY INNOCENT. MAYBE YOU SHOULD LOOK FOR THE PERSON WHO MOVES IN TIME WITH MUSIC.

The _____ did it.

Analyzing characters

Picture This

Words can be used to create images, or pictures, in your mind.
Several items are named below.
Picture each item in your mind.
Then circle the letter of the choice that does *not* help you
create an image of the item.

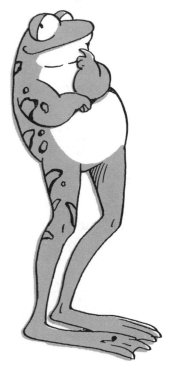

1. an underground cave
   b. darkness
   c. mist
   d. cobwebs
   e. wrinkles

2. a crowded beach
   m. sand castles
   n. falling leaves
   o. colored towels
   p. plastic shovels

3. a car factory
   e. assembly lines
   f. glowing hot metal
   g. palm trees
   h. wheels and doors

4. a jungle
   i. long icicles
   j. warm rain
   k. hanging vines
   l. swarming bugs

5. a library
   l. quiet people
   m. shelves and tables
   n. tennis balls
   o. daily newspapers

6. a carnival
   d. funny performers
   e. frozen dinners
   f. flashing lights
   g. colorful balloons

7. a garbage dump
   b. old papers
   c. noisy trucks
   d. tin cans
   e. new shoes

8. an apple orchard
   q. crisp fruit
   r. clean windows
   s. rows of trees
   t. overloaded baskets

9. a rock band
   s. typewriters
   t. crazy dancing
   u. microphones
   v. loud singing

Can you picture a funny answer to this question?
Write the letters of your choices in order and
"see" what you get.

Q How do trains hear?

A They use their _____.

Forming visual images; using prior knowledge

What Four?

Read each question.
Write your answers on the lines.
When you are finished, compare your answers with
your classmates.

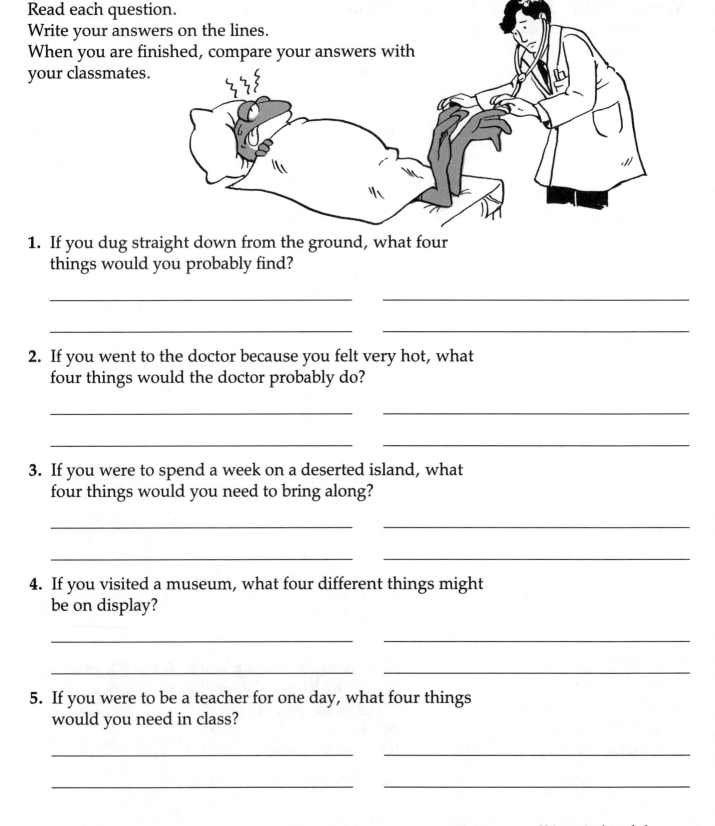

1. If you dug straight down from the ground, what four
   things would you probably find?

   _____   _____

   _____   _____

2. If you went to the doctor because you felt very hot, what
   four things would the doctor probably do?

   _____   _____

   _____   _____

3. If you were to spend a week on a deserted island, what
   four things would you need to bring along?

   _____   _____

   _____   _____

4. If you visited a museum, what four different things might
   be on display?

   _____   _____

   _____   _____

5. If you were to be a teacher for one day, what four things
   would you need in class?

   _____   _____

   _____   _____

Using prior knowledge

ANSWER KEY

MASTER THINKING SKILLS
4

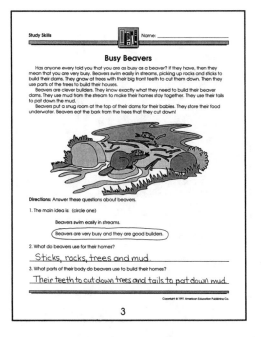

Busy Beavers

Has anyone every told you that you are as busy as a beaver? If they have, then they mean that you are very busy. Beavers swim easily in streams, picking up rocks and sticks to build their dams. They gnaw at trees with their big front teeth to cut them down. Then they use parts of the trees to build their houses.

Beavers are clever builders. They know exactly what they need to build their beaver dams. They use mud from the stream to make their homes stay together. They use their tails to pat down the mud.

Beavers put a snug room at the top of their dams for their babies. They store their food underwater. Beavers eat the bark from the trees that they cut down!

Directions: Answer these questions about beavers.

1. The main idea is: (circle one)

     Beavers swim easily in streams.

     ⟨Beavers are very busy and they are good builders.⟩

2. What do beavers use for their homes?

     Sticks, rocks, trees and mud.

3. What parts of their body do beavers use to build their homes?

     Their teeth to cut down trees and tails to pat down mud.

Copyright © 1991 American Education Publishing Co.

3

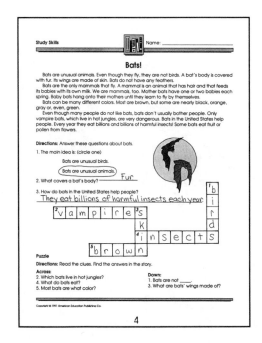

Bats!

Bats are unusual animals. Even though they fly, they are not birds. A bat's body is covered with fur. Its wings are made of skin. Bats do not have any feathers.

Bats are the only mammals that fly. A mammal is an animal that has hair and that feeds its babies with its own milk. We are mammals, too. Mother bats have one or two babies each spring. Baby bats hang onto their mothers until they learn to fly by themselves.

Bats can be many different colors. Most are brown, but some are nearly black, orange, gray or, even, green.

Even though many people do not like bats, bats don't usually bother people. Only vampire bats, which live in hot jungles, are very dangerous. Bats in the United States help people. Every year they eat billions and billions of harmful insects! Some bats eat fruit or pollen from flowers.

Directions: Answer these questions about bats.

1. The main idea is: (circle one)

     Bats are unusual birds.

     ⟨Bats are unusual animals.⟩

2. What covers a bat's body?   Fur

3. How do bats in the United States help people?

     They eat billions of harmful insects each year.

Crossword:
- 1 down: bird (b-i-r-d-s)
- 2 across: vampires
- 3 down: skin (k)
- 4 across: insects
- 5 across: brown

Puzzle

Directions: Read the clues. Find the answers in the story.

Across:
2. Which bats live in hot jungles?
4. What do bats eat?
5. Most bats are what color?

Down:
1. Bats are not ____.
3. What are bats' wings made of?

Copyright © 1991 American Education Publishing Co.

4

73

Name: _____

Blind Bats!

Bats sleep all day because they cannot see well in the bright sunlight. When it they hang upside down in dark places such as barns, caves or hollow trees. As soon as darkness begins to fall, bats wake up. They fly around easily, and fast, at night.

Bats make sounds that help them fly, even though they cannot see well. People cannot hear these sounds. When bats make the sound, it bounces back at them. Bats can tell if something is in their way because there is is an echo. Some people say this is like a radar system!

There are many different kinds of bats, but all of them come out only at night. Some of them fly all night, others fly only in the evening or the early morning. Bats likes to eat at night when they wake up from their long naps.

Many bats eat mosquitoes and moths. But there are some other bats that catch fish swimming in water and eat them. Still other kinds of bats eat birds or mice. Some bats that live in very hot areas eat only some parts of flowers.

Bats that live in cold areas of the country sometimes sleep all winter. That means they hibernate. Other bats that live in cold areas fly to warmer places for the winter!

Directions: Answer these questions about bats.

1. Who cannot hear the sounds bats make? _people_

2. What makes it hard for a bat to see? _bright sunlight_

3. When do bats sleep? _during the day_

4. Where do bats live that eat only parts of flowers?
   In very hot areas.

5. Why do bats make sounds?
   To tell if something is in their way.

6. How do the sounds help them?
   If the sound echoes, the bat can tell that something is in its way.

5

  Name: _____

Easter Eggs, An Old Custom

Coloring Easter Eggs is a tradition that came from a far away country called Poland and other countries near it. People there made beautiful eggs using dye and paints. Today, in America, many people still color Easter Eggs.

The people who started the tradition liked to get rid of the inside of the egg first. To do this, they put a small pin hole in the pointed end of the egg. Then they made a larger pinhole in the other end of the egg. They put the small hole to their mouth and blew out the inside of the egg into a dish.

Today people usually use eggs that have been hardboiled. To decorate them, they use crayons to draw lines around them. Then they add other designs with Easter egg dye or food coloring.

Directions: Answer these questions about decorating eggs.

1. The main idea is: (circle one)

   Making Easter eggs in Poland is messy.

   (People in Poland and other far-away lands started the tradition of making Easter Eggs.)

2. How do they get rid of the inside of the egg?
   They put a small hole in the pointed end of the egg and a larger one in the other end. Then they blow into the smaller end.

3. What is used to decorate Easter Eggs today?
   Crayons and Easter Egg dye or food coloring.

8

  Name: _____

The White House Legend!

Many presidents have lived in the White House in Washington, D.C. Some people say that President Abraham Lincoln still walks there. Even though President Lincoln has been dead for many years, there is still a room there called the Lincoln Bedroom.

Some people say they have seen Lincoln there. Others say they have heard footsteps. One person even said that she saw Lincoln resting on the bed!

But the Lincoln Bedroom is not where President Lincoln slept when he lived at the White House. It is the room where he had meetings with the people who helped him make decisions.

Grace Coolidge was the first person to report seeing Abraham Lincoln. She was the wife of President Calvin Coolidge. Mrs. Coolidge said she saw him looking out the oval window over the main entrance of the White House! Servants at the White House have said that they have seen the him there, too.

Directions: Answer these questions about the White House Legend.

1. The main idea is: (circle one)

   (Some people say President Lincoln is in the White House.)

   President Lincoln stays in the Lincoln Bedroom.

2. Where do people say they have seen or heard the President Lincoln?
   In the area of the Lincoln bedroom.

3. What have people said about the President?
   Some say they have seen him, others heard footsteps, one resting in bed.

4. Where did Mrs. Coolidge say she saw the President?
   In the window over the main entrance of the White House.

6

  Name: _____

Using Chopsticks!

Oriental people have eaten their food with chopsticks for many years. Chopsticks are two thin pieces of wood that are almost pointed on one end.

Chopsticks were used in China thousands of years ago. Ivory, gold or silver chopsticks were even used for special occasions. People who used chopsticks to eat with were considered very smart!

Today even American people sometimes like to use chopsticks! But using chopsticks is not easy. Both chopsticks are held in one hand.

A person holds one chopstick between his thumb and finger. This chopstick is not supposed to move. The other fingers help moved the other chopstick. Chopsticks are an old custom with people from Oriental countries such as China and Japan. But they use forks and knives, too!

Directions: Answer these questions about chopsticks.

1. Who used chopsticks first? _Some Chinese people._

2. What are chopsticks? _Two thin pieces of wood._

3. When did the Chinese start using chopsticks?
   Thousands of years ago.

4. Where are chopsticks also used today?
   In America and in Oriental countries.

5. Why is it hard to use chopsticks?
   Because both sticks are held in one hand to pick up food.

6. How do chopsticks work?
   One stick stays still while the other helps pick up food.

9

  Name: _____

Mr. Lincoln

Abraham Lincoln was president of the United States from 1861 to 1865. He was president when the war between the North and the South started. That war divided the United States into two parts. It made Abraham Lincoln very sad. It was called the Civil War.

Abraham Lincoln hated to see the country being hurt by war. He did not want people fighting each other and dying. The United States was split because many of the states in the South wanted to have slavery. Abraham Lincoln was against slavery.

He made a famous speech called the Gettysburg Address. Abraham Lincoln wanted to make sure that the United States stayed one country. It made him very unhappy that some of the states in the South wanted to make another country.

Finally, in 1865 the war was over. The South decided to become part of the United States again. Abraham Lincoln was very happy!

Only 11 days after the war was over Lincoln was killed. He was watching a play at a theater in Washington, D.C. when a man named John Wilkes Booth shot him. He died the next morning on April 15, 1865.

Directions: Answer these questions about Abraham Lincoln.

1. Who was president from 1861-1865? _Abraham Lincoln_

2. What happened while Lincoln was president?
   The war between the North and the South started.

3. When was the war over?
   Just before Lincoln was shot in 1865.

4. Where did Lincoln give his famous speech? _At Gettysburg._

5. Why was the war over?
   The South decided to become part of the United States again.

6. How long was it until Lincoln died? _Only 11 days._

7

  Name: _____

Review

Worry Beads!

Sometimes when Greek people have problems they work with their worry beads. Worry beads are an old custom from Greece. They help people become calm by counting or moving the beads.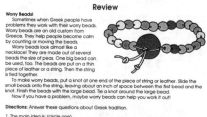

Worry beads look almost like a necklace! They are made out of several beads the size of peas. One big bead can be used, too. The beads are put on a thin piece of leather or a string. Then the string is tied together.

To make worry beads, put a knot at one end of the piece of string or leather. Slide the small beads onto the string, leaving about an inch of space between the first bead and the knot. Finish the beads with the large bead. Tie a knot around the large bead.

Now if you have a problem, maybe worry beads can help you work it out!

Directions: Answer these questions about Greek tradition.

1. The main idea is: (circle one)

   (Worry beads are a Greek custom.)

   Worry beads do not look like a necklace.

2. Who uses worry beads? _Some Greek people._

3. What are worry beads?
   A string of beads put together like a necklace.

4. When do people use worry beads? _When they have problems._

5. Where did that custom come from? _Greece._

6. Why do worry beads help people?
   They help make them calm.

7. How are worry beads used?
   People count them or move them on the string.

10

A Man Walks on the Moon!

"That's one small step for a man, one giant leap for mankind."

That is what Neil Armstrong said when he stepped onto the moon in 1969. Neil Armstrong was the first person to walk on the moon. He was an astronaut who had been in space once before.

This time, though, he went into space with two other astronauts. While one of them circled the moon with part of the spaceship, Armstrong and another astronaut landed on the moon in a special part of the spaceship. That special section was called "Eagle."

Neil Armstrong stepped onto the moon first. While he was doing it, he said the words that are written above. People throughout the world were able to watch on television as Armstrong took his first moon steps!

Armstrong and the other astronaut, Edwin Aldrin, spent more than two hours on the moon. They took pictures. They set up experiments. They even collected rocks!

The two astronauts gathered information that others used in trips to the moon later on.

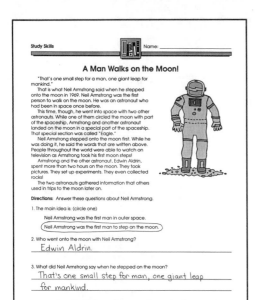

Directions: Answer these questions about Neil Armstrong.

1. The main idea is: (circle one)

Neil Armstrong was the first man in outer space.

(Neil Armstrong was the first man to step on the moon.)

2. Who went onto the moon with Neil Armstrong?
Edwin Aldrin.

3. What did Neil Armstrong say when he stepped on the moon?
That's one small step for man, one giant leap for mankind.

11

The Moon

The moon floats around the Earth. It is called a satellite. It is very different from the Earth. It has a lot of rocks and dust on it. Craters are big holes on the moon. There are no plants or animals on the moon. Some of the moon's rocks are glassy. They seem to have many different colors in them.

There is no wind or rain on the moon. The footprints that Neil Armstrong and Edwin Aldrin left on the moon will be there for a long time because the dust does not blow around.

Earth has only one moon. Other planets have more moons. Scientists think that Jupiter has at least 14 moons. Saturn has the largest moon, though. It is called Titan. People on Earth have been studying the moon for many years. Man-made satellites float around in space taking pictures of the moon. Scientists study the pictures looking for clues about the moon.

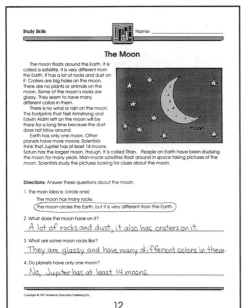

Directions: Answer these questions about the moon.

1. The main idea is: (circle one)

The moon has many rocks.

(The moon circles the Earth, but it is very different from the Earth.)

2. What does the moon have on it?
A lot of rocks and dust, it also has craters on it.

3. What are some moon rocks like?
They are glassy and have many different colors in them.

4. Do planets have only one moon?
No, Jupiter has at least 14 moons.

12

Circling the Earth!

John Glenn was the first American to circle the Earth. When someone circles the Earth it is called "orbiting."

It was on February 20, 1962, when John Glenn went into space and started the trip around the Earth. The name of his spaceship was "Friendship 7."

Other American astronauts had already been into space. They knew what it was like to have no gravity. Their work helped John Glenn when he took his flight into space. John Glenn went around the Earth all by himself. He was the only astronaut on board "Friendship 7"!

John Glenn was not the first person to orbit the Earth, though. The year before he went around the Earth, a Russian man did it. Yuri Gagarin was the first person to travel around the Earth.

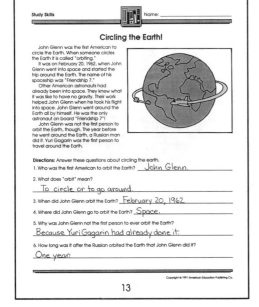

Directions: Answer these questions about circling the earth.

1. Who was the first American to orbit the Earth? John Glenn.

2. What does "orbit" mean?
To circle or to go around.

3. When did John Glenn orbit the Earth? February 20, 1962

4. Where did John Glenn go to orbit the Earth? Space.

5. Why was John Glenn not the first person to ever orbit the Earth?
Because Yuri Gagarin had already done it.

6. How long was it after the Russian orbited the Earth that John Glenn did it?
One year

13

Chimponauts Went First!

Chimpanzees went into space before astronauts! In the 1950s, scientists decided to try sending chimps into space because they were much like humans but they were stronger.

The first chimps to ride in a rocket were two named Pat and Mike. Their ride was in 1953. But Ham was the first chimpanzee to go into space. That was in 1961.

Before John Glenn orbited the earth, a chimpanzee had already done it. The chimp, named Enos, had circled the earth twice!

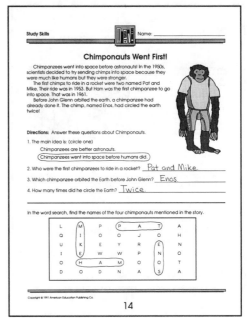

Directions: Answer these questions about Chimponauts.

1. The main idea is: (circle one)

Chimpanzees are better astronauts.

(Chimpanzees went into space before humans did.)

2. Who were the first chimpanzees to ride in a rocket? Pat and Mike.

3. Which chimpanzee orbited the Earth before John Glenn? Enos.

4. How many times did he circle the Earth? Twice.

In the word search, find the names of the four chimponauts mentioned in the story.

L	M	P	A	T	A
Q	I	O	O	J	H
U	K	E	Y	R	N
K	E	W	W	P	E
O	H	A	M	O	O
D	O	D	N	A	S

14

Sally Ride, First Woman in Space

Sally Ride was the first American woman in space. She was only 31 years old when she went into space in 1982. She was also the youngest person to go into space!

A lot of people want to be astronauts. When Sally Ride was chosen there were 8,000 people who wanted to be in the class. Only 35 people were picked. Six of those people were women.

Sally Ride rode in the space ship "Challenger." She was called a mission specialist. Like any astronaut, Sally Ride had to study for a couple years before she went into space. She spent six days on her journey. Sally Ride has even written a book for children about her adventure! It is called To Space and Back.

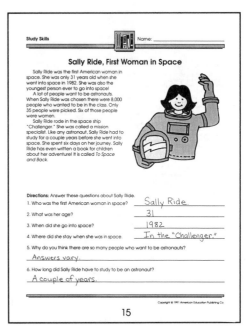

Directions: Answer these questions about Sally Ride.

1. Who was the first American woman in space? Sally Ride.

2. What was her age? 31

3. When did she go into space? 1982

4. Where did she stay when she was in space. In the "Challenger."

5. Why do you think there are so many people who want to be astronauts?
Answers vary.

6. How long did Sally Ride have to study to be an astronaut?
A couple of years.

15

Floating in Space!

Life in space is very different than it is on Earth. There is no gravity in space. Gravity is what holds us to the ground. In space, everything floats around.

Astronauts wear suction cups on their shoes to hold them to the floor. At night they do not crawl into bed like you do. Instead, they climb into sleeping bags that hang on the wall and then they zip themselves in. If an astronaut wants a drink of water, he cannot just pour himself a glass. The water would form little balls that would float around the spaceship! Instead, water has to be squirted into the astronauts' mouths from bottles or containers.

When astronauts are in space they do a lot of floating around outside their spaceship. Astronauts always have special jobs to do in space. One astronaut is the pilot of the spaceship. The other astronauts do experiments and gather information about their trip.

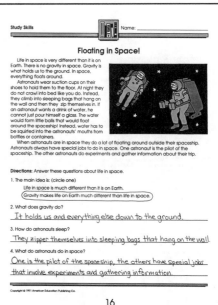

Directions: Answer these questions about life in space.

1. The main idea is: (circle one)

Life in space is much different than it is on Earth.

(Gravity makes life on Earth much different than life in space.)

2. What does gravity do?
It holds us and everything else down to the ground.

3. How do astronauts sleep?
They zipper themselves into sleeping bags that hang on the wall.

4. What do astronauts do in space?
One is the pilot of the spaceship, the others have special jobs that involve experiments and gathering information.

16

The Future of Space Study

People in charge of the space program in the United States want to keep studying space. They plan to look at the sun and some of the planets in the solar system.

They are interested in exploring Jupiter and all its moons. They also want to look at Venus, which is Earth's neighbor.

Soon they want to build a space station where people can stay while they do some studies. The space station will include places to live, laboratories for experiments, and collectors for solar energy from the sun. People will be able to live in the space station to do long studies and experiments. Scientists say that one day people will be able to live in space all their lives. Some space cities have already been designed!

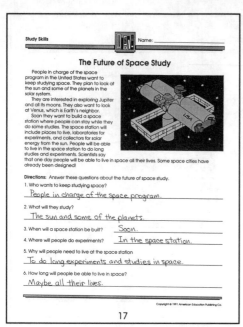

Directions: Answer these questions about the future of space study.

1. Who wants to keep studying space?

   People in charge of the space program.

2. What will they study?

   The sun and some of the planets.

3. When will a space station be built? Soon.

4. Where will people do experiments? In the space station.

5. Why will people need to live at the space station

   To do long experiments and studies in space.

6. How long will people be able to live in space?

   Maybe all their lives.

17

Review

Early Ideas about Space

People have dreamed about going into space for hundreds of years. There are legends that tell about inventors who wanted to get birds to fly to the moon. In 1864 a French author named Jules Verne wrote a book called, *From the Earth to the Moon*. In the book he wrote about men being shot into space from a huge gun.

Jules Verne made up that story. Other writers also made up stories about going to the moon. It was during the 1920s that several scientists wrote about sending rockets into space. They decided that liquid fuel was needed. Since then space exploration has come a long way!

A Russian named Aleksei Leonov was the first person in space. An American, Edwin White, went into space next. Both men did experiments that later helped other astronauts in their trips to outer space!

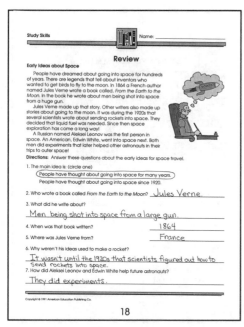

Directions: Answer these questions about the early ideas for space travel.

1. The main idea is: (circle one)

   (People have thought about going into space for many years.)

   People have thought about going into space since 1920.

2. Who wrote a book called *From the Earth to the Moon*? Jules Verne.

3. What did he write about?

   Men being shot into space from a large gun.

4. When was that book written? 1864

5. Where was Jules Verne from? France

6. Why weren't his ideas used to make a rocket?

   It wasn't until the 1920s that scientists figured out how to send rockets into space.

7. How did Aleksei Leonov and Edwin White help future astronauts?

   They did experiments.

18

Taking Notes

Taking notes is important because it helps you understand what you read or hear. Everyone has his or her own way of taking notes. Here are some things you should remember when taking notes:

✔ Use whole sentences or short phrases.
✔ Make words shorter to save time. For example, "discovery" could become "disc" in your notes.
✔ If you use the same name often in your notes, use initials. For example, George Washington could become G.W.
✔ Be brief, but make sure you can understand you notes.
✔ Number your notes so you can understand where each note starts and stops.

Directions: Do the exercise about taking notes.

Use a piece of paper to cover the story about penguins. Now read the questions. Think about them. Read the story about penguins. Take some notes on another piece of paper that could help you answer the questions.

1. Why are penguins unusual?
2. Do penguins swim?
3. Where do penguins live?
4. Do penguins lay eggs like other birds?

Penguins are Unusual Birds

Penguins may be the most unusual birds. They cannot fly. But they can swim very fast through ice cold water. They can dive deep into the water and they can jump high out of it. Some penguins make their nests out of rocks instead of twigs and grass. Penguins live in very cold parts of the country. Unlike other birds, they only lay one egg at a time.

Right after a mother penguin lays her egg she waddles back to the ocean. The father penguin holds the egg in his feet, covering it with part of his stomach to keep the egg warm. When the egg is ready to hatch, the mother penguin returns. Then the father penguin takes a turn looking for food.

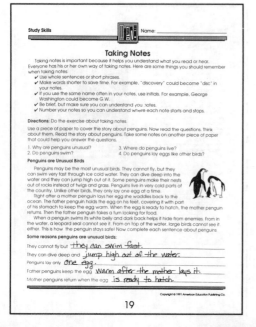

When a penguin swims its white belly and dark back helps it hide from enemies. From in the water, a leopard seal cannot see it. From on top of the water, large birds cannot see it either. This is how the penguin stays safe! Now complete each sentence about penguins.

Some reasons penguins are unusual birds:

They cannot fly but they can swim fast.

They can dive deep and jump high out of the water.

Penguins lay only one egg.

Father penguins keep the egg warm after the mother lays it.

Mother penguins return when the egg is ready to hatch.

19

76

Taking Notes

Directions: Cover the story about raisins with a piece of paper. Look at the questions. Then read the story. Take some notes that help you answer the questions.

1. How do grapes become raisins?
2. How are grapes dried?
3. Why are raisins brown?
4. What makes raisins sweet?

From Grapes to Raisins!

Grapes grow well in places that have a lot of sun. In the United States, California is a big producer of grapes and raisins. When grapes are plump and round, they can be picked from their vines to be made into raisins. After the grapes are picked they are put on big wooden or paper trays. They sit in the sun for many days.

Slowly the grapes begin to dry and turn into wrinkled raisins. The sun causes them to change colors. Grapes turn brown as they become raisins. Machines take the stems off of the raisins. Then the raisins are washed. After being dried again, they are put into boxes.

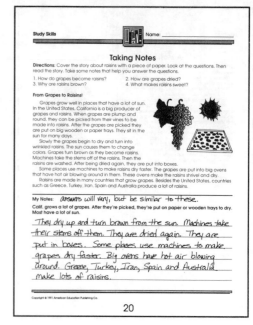

Some places use machines to make raisins dry faster. The grapes are put into big ovens that have hot air blowing around in them. These ovens make the raisins shrivel and dry.

Raisins are made in many countries that grow grapes. Besides the United States, countries such as Greece, Turkey, Iran, Spain and Australia produce a lot of raisins.

My Notes: answers will vary, but be similar to these.

Calif. grows a lot of grapes. After they're picked, they're put on paper or wooden trays to dry. Most have a lot of sun.

They dry up and turn brown from the sun. Machines take their stems off them. They are dried again. They are put in boxes. Some places use machines to make grapes dry faster. Big ovens have hot air blowing around. Greece, Turkey, Iran, Spain and Australia make lots of raisins.

20

Taking Notes

Directions: Cover the story about Graham crackers with a sheet of paper. Look at the questions. Then read the story about Graham crackers. After that, write some notes that could help you answer the questions.

1. Where did Graham crackers come from?
2. Who invented Graham crackers?
3. What are Graham crackers made of?
4. Why were Graham crackers made?

Graham Crackers

Graham crackers were invented around 1830. A minister named Sylvester Graham wanted people to eat healthier foods. He did not think that people should eat meat or white bread. He wanted people to eat more fruits and vegetables and wheat breads that are brown instead of white.

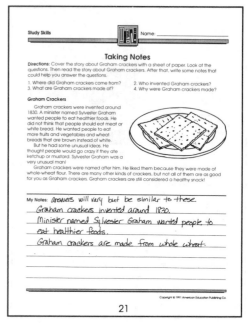

But he had some unusual ideas. He thought people would go crazy if they ate ketchup or mustard. Sylvester Graham was a very unusual man!

Graham crackers were named after him. He liked them because they were made of whole-wheat flour. There are many other kinds of crackers, but not all of them are as good for you as Graham crackers. Graham crackers are still considered a healthy snack!

My Notes: answers will vary but be similar to these.

Graham crackers invented around 1830.

Minister named Sylvester Graham wanted people to eat healthier foods.

Graham crackers are made from whole wheat.

21

Taking Notes

Directions: Before you read the story about the history of soccer, ask yourself some questions. For example, "Where is the game from?"

Now read the story. Take some notes that help you answer your questions.

My questions: questions will vary
1. Where did the game come from?
2. How is soccer played?
3. How many players are on a team?
4. How old is the game?

Soccer: An Ancient Game

Soccer is a very old game. It was played thousands of years ago, but the rules varied and everyone played the game differently. By the mid-1800s soccer was a popular sport in England. Everyone still had different rules for the game, however.

In 1863 the Football Association was formed to make standard rules. The Football Association decided that wild kicking was not allowed during the game. The people who liked to kick the ball wildly got together and made their own game. It is called rugby!

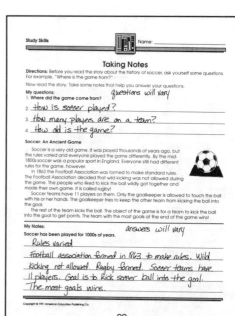

Soccer teams have 11 players on them. Only the goalkeeper is allowed to touch the ball with his or her hands. The goalkeeper tries to keep the other team from kicking the ball into the goal.

The rest of the team kicks the ball. The object of the game is for a team to kick the ball into the goal to get points. The team with the most goals at the end of the game wins!

My Notes: answers will vary

Soccer has been played for 1000s of years.

Rules varied

Football association formed in 1863 to make rules. Wild kicking not allowed. Rugby formed. Soccer teams have 11 players. Goal is to kick soccer ball into the goal. The most goals wins.

22

Taking Notes

Directions: Before you read about the game called cricket, write a few questions that you would ask about it. Then read the story. Take notes to answer those questions.

My questions: *questions will vary*
1. What is cricket?
2. When did cricket start?
3. *Where is it played?*
4. *How is it played?*

Cricket: English Baseball?

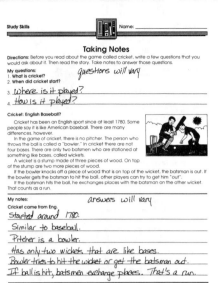

Cricket has been an English sport since at least 1780. Some people say it is like American baseball. There are many differences, however.

In the game of cricket, there is no pitcher. The person who throws the ball is called a "bowler." In cricket there are not four bases. There are only two batsmen who are stationed at something like bases, called wickets.

A wicket is a stump made of three pieces of wood. On top of the stump are two more pieces of wood.

If the bowler knocks off a piece of wood that is on top of the wicket, the batsman is out. If the bowler gets the batsman to hit the ball, other players can try to get him "out". If the batsman hits the ball, he exchanges places with the batsman on the other wicket. That counts as a run.

My notes: *answers will vary*
Cricket came from Eng.
Started around 1780.
Similar to baseball.
Pitcher is a bowler.
Has only two wickets that are like bases.
Bowler tries to hit the wicket or get the batsman out.
If ball is hit, batsmen exchange places. That's a run.

Copyright © 1991 American Education Publishing Co.

23

Taking Notes

Directions: This is a story about how skateboards were first made. Before you read the story, write a few questions that you may want to answer. Then read the story. Take a few notes to help you answer those questions.

My questions: *questions will vary*
1. How were skateboards first made?
2. *Who used skateboards?*
3. *Why did they want to use a skateboard?*
4. *What was used to make skateboards?*

From Skates to Boards!

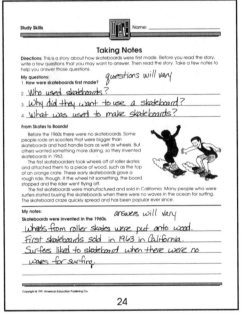

Before the 1960s there were no skateboards. Some people rode on scooters that were bigger than skateboards and had handle bars as well as wheels. But others wanted something more daring, so they invented skateboards in 1963.

The first skateboards took wheels off of roller skates and attached them to a piece of wood, such as the top of an orange crate. These early skateboards gave a rough ride, though. If the wheel hit something, the board stopped and the rider went flying off.

The first skateboards were manufactured and sold in California. Many people who were surfers started buying the skateboards when there were no waves in the ocean for surfing. The skateboard craze quickly spread and has been popular ever since.

My notes: *answers will vary*
Skateboards were invented in the 1960s.
Wheels from roller skates were put onto wood.
First skateboards sold in 1963 in California.
Surfers liked to skateboard when there were no waves for surfing.

Copyright © 1991 American Education Publishing Co.

24

Taking Notes

Directions: Here is a story about the interesting and funny history of roller skating. Write a few questions before you read the story. Read the story and take some notes that will answer your questions.

My questions: *questions will vary*
1. When were roller skates invented?
2. *Why were they funny?*
3. *Why did people like roller skates?*

A Humorous Skating Story

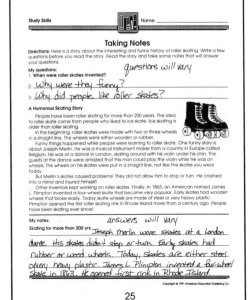

People have been roller skating for more than 200 years. The idea to roller skate came from people who liked to ice skate. Ice skating is older than roller skating.

In the beginning, roller skates were made with two or three wheels in a straight line. The wheels were either wooden or rubber.

Funny things happened while people were learning to roller skate. One funny story is about Joseph Merlin. He was a musical instrument maker from a country in Europe called Belgium. He was at a dance in London, skating around with his violin under his chin. The guests at the dance were amazed that this man could play the violin while he was on wheels. The wheels on his skates were put in a straight line, not like the skates you wear today.

But Merlin's skates caused problems! They did not allow him to stop or turn. He crashed into a mirror and injured himself!

Other inventors kept working on roller skates. Finally, in 1863, an American named James L. Plimpton invented a four-wheel skate that became very popular. Early skates had wooden wheels that broke easily. Today skate wheels are made of steel or very heavy plastic. Plimpton opened the first roller skating rink in Rhode Island more than a century ago. People have been skating ever since!

My notes: *answers will vary*
Skating for more than 200 yrs. *Joseph Merlin wore skates at a London dance. His skates didn't stop or turn. Early skates had rubber or wood wheels. Today, skates are either steel or very heavy plastic. James L. Plimpton invented a four-wheel skate in 1863. He opened first rink in Rhode Island.*

Copyright © 1991 American Education Publishing Co.

25

Review

Directions: Before you read about why people started ice skating, write a few questions that you would like to answer. Then read the story. Take notes to answer your questions.

My questions: *questions will vary*
1. Why did people start skating?
2. *How did they get the idea to ice skate?*
3. *What were their ice skates made from?*
4. *Where did they live?*

Why did People Start Ice Skating?

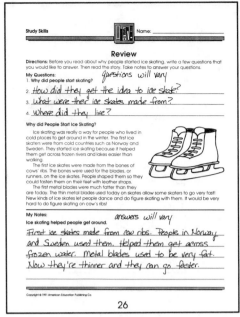

Ice skating was really a way for people who lived in cold places to get around in the winter. The first ice skaters were from cold countries such as Norway and Sweden. They started ice skating because it helped them get across frozen rivers and lakes easier than walking.

The first ice skates were made from the bones of cows' ribs. The bones were used for the blades, or runners, on the ice skates. People shaped them so they could fasten them on their feet with leather straps.

The first metal blades were much fatter than they are today. The thin metal blades used today on skates allow some skaters to go very fast! New kinds of ice skates let people dance and do figure skating with them. It would be very hard to do figure skating on cow's ribs!

My Notes: *answers will vary*
Ice skating helped people get around.
First ice skates made from cow ribs. People in Norway and Sweden used them. Helped them get across frozen water. Metal blades used to be very fat. Now they're thinner and they can go faster.

Copyright © 1991 American Education Publishing Co.

26

Outlining

Outlines are plans that help you organize your thoughts. If you are writing a paper, an outline helps you decide what to write about. An outline should look similar to this:

An Outline

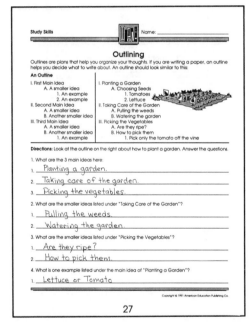

I. First Main Idea
  A. A smaller idea
    1. An example
    2. An example
II. Second Main Idea
  A. A smaller idea
  B. Another smaller idea
III. Third Main Idea
  A. A smaller idea
  B. Another smaller idea
    1. An example

I. Planting a Garden
  A. Choosing Seeds
    1. Tomatoes
    2. Lettuce
II. Taking Care of the Garden
  A. Pulling the weeds
  B. Watering the garden
III. Picking the Vegetables
  A. Are they ripe?
  B. How to pick them
    1. Pick only the tomato off the vine

Directions: Look at the outline on the right about how to plant a garden. Answer the questions.

1. What are the 3 main ideas here:
1. *Planting a garden.*
2. *Taking care of the garden.*
3. *Picking the vegetables.*

2. What are the smaller ideas listed under "Taking Care of the Garden"?
1. *Pulling the weeds.*
2. *Watering the garden.*

3. What are the smaller ideas listed under "Picking the Vegetables"?
1. *Are they ripe?*
2. *How to pick them.*

4. What is one example listed under the main idea of "Planting a Garden"?
1. *Lettuce or Tomato*

Copyright © 1991 American Education Publishing Co.

27

Outlining

Directions: Look at the sample outline about building a house. Then follow the instructions to complete your own outline.

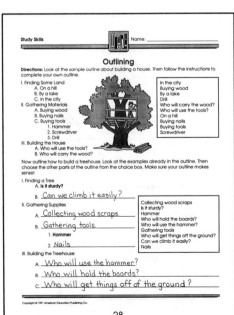

I. Finding Some Land
  A. On a hill
  B. By a lake
  C. In the city
II. Gathering Materials
  A. Buying wood
  B. Buying nails
  C. Buying tools
    1. Hammer
    2. Screwdriver
    3. Drill
III. Building the House
  A. Who will use the tools?
  B. Who will carry the wood?

In the city
Buying wood
By a lake
Drill
Who will carry the wood?
Who will use the tools?
On a hill
Buying nails
Buying tools
Screwdriver

Now outline how to build a treehouse. Look at the examples already in the outline. Then choose the other parts of the outline from the choice box. Make sure your outline makes sense!

I. Finding a Tree
  A. Is it sturdy?
  B. *Can we climb it easily?*
II. Gathering Supplies
  A. *Collecting wood scraps.*
  B. *Gathering tools.*
    1. *Hammer*
    2. *Nails*
III. Building the Treehouse
  A. *Who will use the hammer?*
  B. *Who will hold the boards?*
  C. *Who will get things off of the ground?*

Collecting wood scraps
Is it sturdy?
Hammer
Who will hold the boards?
Who will use the hammer?
Gathering tools
Who will get things off the ground?
Can we climb it easily?
Nails

Copyright © 1991 American Education Publishing Co.

28

Page 29

Outlining

Directions: Make an outline of what you need to do once your tree house is built. Fill in the spaces in the outline with phrases from the choice box.

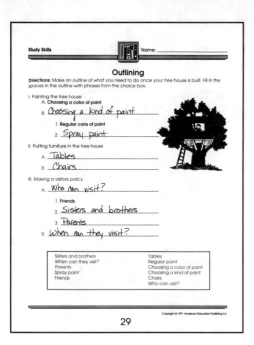

I. Painting the tree house
  A. Choosing a color of paint
  B. _Choosing a kind of paint_
    1. Regular cans of paint
    2. _Spray paint_

II. Putting furniture in the tree house
  A. _Tables_
  B. _Chairs_

III. Making a visitors policy
  A. _Who can visit?_
    1. Friends
    2. _Sisters and brothers_
    3. _Parents_
  B. _When can they visit?_

Sisters and brothers	Tables
When can they visit?	Regular paint
Parents	Choosing a color of paint
Spray paint	Choosing a kind of paint
Friends	Chairs
	Who can visit?

Page 32

The Mayflower's Voyage

The Mayflower ship left England in 1620. Carrying 101 passengers. Some of those passengers were called pilgrims. Pilgrims are people who had wandered from country to country looking for a place to make their home. It took 66 days to cross the Atlantic. The ship was crowded. There were some accidents on board. The Mayflower landed at the tip of Cape Cod in Massachusetts. Several men searched the area to find the best place to start a colony. They finally settled on Plymouth. The pilgrims lived on the Mayflower through the winter. The Mayflower returned to England in April, 1621. None of the pilgrims went back with it.

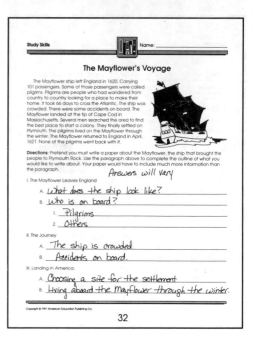

Directions: Pretend you must write a paper about the Mayflower, the ship that brought the people to Plymouth Rock. Use the paragraph above to complete the outline of what you would like to write about. Your paper would have to include much more information than the paragraph.

Answers will vary

I. The Mayflower Leaves England
  A. _What does the ship look like?_
  B. _Who is on board?_
    1. _Pilgrims_
    2. _Others_

II. The Journey
  A. _The ship is crowded_
  B. _Accidents on board._

III. Landing in America.
  A. _Choosing a site for the settlement_
  B. _Living aboard the Mayflower through the winter._

Page 30

Christopher Columbus's Voyage

Long ago people in Europe believed the world was flat. They thought that if anyone set sail and did not turn around to come back that they would drop off of the Earth! Christopher Columbus did not believe that. He thought the world was round and he wanted to set sail to prove that. Christopher Columbus wanted the King of Portugal to give him the money for his journey but the king would not. Neither would the kings of England or France. Finally Queen Isabella, of Spain, sent Columbus the money.

With this money Columbus got three ships: the *Pinta*, the *Nina* and the *Santa Maria*. Columbus recruited about 90 sailors from Spain for the voyage in 1492. During their voyage there were many problems with the ships that had to be repaired. Some of the sailors wanted to go back to Spain. They even talked about throwing Columbus overboard and heading home!

Finally Columbus and his sailors spotted land. Columbus thought it was India, but it was really the West Indies, a small group of islands in the Atlantic Ocean. The natives that lived there were friendly. Columbus gave them strings of beads and they gave Columbus and his sailors some tobacco.

Directions: Use phrases from the choice box to complete the outline about Columbus.

I. Christopher Columbus's Ideas
  A. The world was round
  B. _The Queen of Spain would give him money_

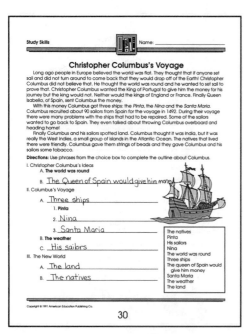

II. Columbus's Voyage
  A. _Three ships_
    1. Pinta
    2. _Nina_
    3. _Santa Maria_
  B. The weather
  C. _His sailors_

III. The New World
  A. _The land_
  B. _The natives_

The natives
Pinta
His sailors
Nina
The world was round
Three ships
The queen of Spain would give him money
Santa Maria
The weather
The land

Page 33

Outlining

The First Thanksgiving

The pilgrims got to Plymouth Rock just as winter set in. Many people died that winter from the cold and from having no food. The following spring, the pilgrims started planting vegetable gardens. An Indian named Squanto helped them. They planted peas, wheat, beans, corn and pumpkins. When fall came, the pilgrims were so glad to have enough food they invited the Indians to share their first Thanksgiving. In addition to things from their garden, they also shared wild geese that they had killed and other food such as sweet potatoes and fresh berries that they had fixed.

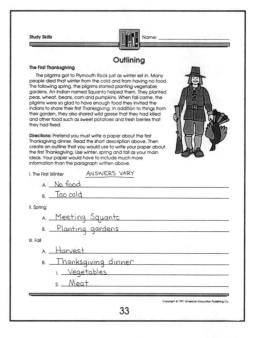

Directions: Pretend you must write a paper about the first Thanksgiving dinner. Read the short description above. Then create an outline that you would use to write your paper about the first Thanksgiving. Use winter, spring and fall as your main ideas. Your paper would have to include much more information than the paragraph written above.

I. The First Winter   _ANSWERS VARY_
  A. _No food_
  B. _Too cold_

II. Spring
  A. _Meeting Squanto_
  B. _Planting gardens_

III. Fall
  A. _Harvest_
  B. _Thanksgiving dinner_
    1. _Vegetables_
    2. _Meat_

Page 31

Sally Ride's Ride

Sally Ride was the first American woman in space. She was one of only six women in her class and she was only 31 years old. Sally Ride wanted to go into space because she was curious. Before she left for her journey, though, she had to go to school for several months. She also had to do many physical activities that would make her body strong enough to handle the long trip.

When Sally Ride's space rocket took off, she was the only woman aboard. She spent many days doing tests and experiments about outer space with the other astronauts on board with her. She also got to see what it was like to live without gravity. She had to eat different food and sleep in a different position. Still, Sally Ride enjoyed her trip into space!

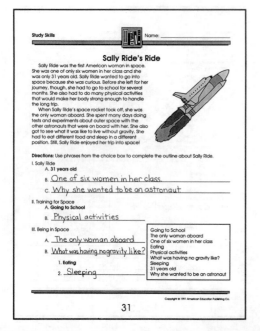

Directions: Use phrases from the choice box to complete the outline about Sally Ride.

I. Sally Ride
  A. 31 years old
  B. _One of six women in her class._
  C. _Why she wanted to be an astronaut_

II. Training for Space
  A. Going to School
  B. _Physical activities_

III. Being in Space
  A. _The only woman aboard_
  B. _What was having no gravity like?_
    1. Eating
    2. _Sleeping_

Going to School
The only woman aboard
One of six women in her class
Eating
Physical activities
What was having no gravity like?
Sleeping
31 years old
Why she wanted to be an astronaut

Page 34

Review

Pocahontas

Pocahontas was an Indian princess born in 1595, the daughter of the Indian Chief Powhatan. Powhatan had many children but Pocahontas was said to be his favorite. Her name meant "bright stream between two hills."

When Pocahontas was only 12 years old she met an Englishman named Captain John Smith. Smith had been taken prisoner by some of the Indians. It is said that Pocahontas saved his life when the Indians tried to kill him. Pocahontas liked to hear stories about the English and John Smith made many gifts for her. Many times she tried to make peace between the Indians and the Englishman. After John Smith went back to England, Pocahontas met and married another Englishman named John Rolfe. Together they had a son. They lived in England for a while, where Pocahontas was treated very well. Just as they were preparing to return to America, Pocahontas became ill. She died of pneumonia in 1617 when she was only 22 years old.

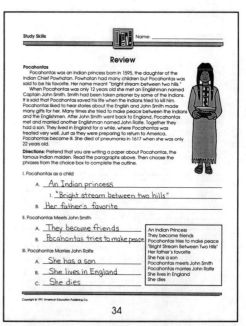

Directions: Pretend that you are writing a paper about Pocahontas, the famous Indian maiden. Read the paragraphs above. Then choose the phrases from the choice box to complete the outline.

I. Pocahontas as a child
  A. _An Indian princess_
    1. _"Bright stream between two hills"_
  B. _Her father's favorite_

II. Pocahontas Meets John Smith
  A. _They become friends_
  B. _Pocahontas tries to make peace_

III. Pocahontas Marries John Rolfe
  A. _She has a son_
  B. _She lives in England_
  C. _She dies_

An Indian Princess
They become friends
Pocahontas tries to make peace
"Bright Stream Between Two Hills"
Her father's favorite
She has a son
Pocahontas meets John Smith
Pocahontas marries John Rolfe
She lives in England
She dies

Library Skills

Every book in a library is listed in a library catalog. Most library catalogs are drawers full of file cards. Here is an example of a card from a library catalog.

The card catalog helps you find the book you are looking for. Card catalogs list books by their **titles**, their **authors** and their **subjects**. All three of these listings are in ABC order.

For example, if you wanted to find a book titled, *Pocahontas, An Indian Princess*, you would look under P in the card catalog. If you wanted to find other books about Pocahontas, you would also look under P to find others written on that subject. Or, if you knew the name of an author who had written a book about Pocahontas, you could find a card on the book by looking in the card catalog under the author's name.

Many libraries have begun using computers instead of card catalogs. You can use a computer to find books, too. Finding books in a library is not hard if you learn how to use the card catalog!

```
970.2
G89a        INDIANS
            Gridley, Marion E.
            American Indian Women
            Hawthorn Books, Inc. 1979
```

Directions: Answer the questions about using a card catalog.

1. To find the book *American Indian Women*, would you look under the author card, title card or subject card? — *Title cards*
2. You would like to find a book about the Cherokee Indians. Which kind of card would you find? — *Subject cards*
3. The book you want to find is called *Animals of Long Ago*. Which kind of card would you find? — *Title cards*
4. You know that Marion E. Gridley has written books about Indians. You want to read one of her books. Which kind of cards would you use? — *Author cards*
5. You want to find some books about the moon. Which kind of cards would you use? — *Subject cards*
6. You want to find the book *Easy Microwave Cooking for Kids*. Which card would you find? — *Title cards*
7. Diana Reische has written a book about the pilgrims. Which kind of card would you find? — *Author cards*
8. You want help finding out how to use the library. Which kind of cards would you find? — *Subject cards*
9. You want information about the White House where the president lives. Which kind of cards would you find? — *Subject cards*
10. You want to find Claire McInerney's books. Which kind of cards would you find? — *Author cards*

35

Library Skills

Directions: Read about the Dewey Decimal System. Then follow the instructions.

Using a card catalog helps you find the book that you want. All nonfiction books — except biographies — are filed according to their number. (Nonfiction books are books based on facts. Biographies are true books that tell about people's lives.)

These numbers are part of the Dewey Decimal System. They are called **call numbers**. Each card in a card catalog will have a book's **call number** on it. Look at the example below.

```
919.8
B85e        Bringle, Mary.
            Eskimos. F. Watts. 1973
```

All libraries using the Dewey Decimal System follow the same pattern for filing books. The System divides all nonfiction books into 10 main groups, each represented by numbers.

0-099	General works such as libraries, computers, etc.
100-199	Philosophy
200-299	Religion
300-399	Social Sciences
400-499	Language
500-599	Pure Science such as math, astronomy, chemistry, etc.
600-699	Applied Science such as medicine, engineering, etc.
700-799	Arts and Recreation
800-899	Literature
900-999	History

Each book has a specific call number. For example, a book about ghosts could be 133.1.

Look at where some subjects fall in the Dewey Decimal System.

Pets	630	Maps	910
Baseball	796	Monsters	791
Butterflies	595	Mummies	390
Cooking	640	Presidents	920
Dinosaurs	560	Space	620
Fairy Tales	390	Trees	580

Write the Dewey Decimal Number under which the following books would be found at the library.

560 Animals of Long Ago   *920* Our American Presidents
590 City Leaves *City Trees*   *390* Mummies Made in Egypt
640 Easy Microwave Cooking for Kids   *791* Real-Life Monsters
620 To Space and Back   *390* Peter Rabbit
796 Amazing Baseball Teams   *910* The Children's Atlas

38

Library Skills

Directions: Look at the list of authors, subjects and titles. Write **A** for an author, write **S** if it is a subject and write **T** if it is a title. Sort each into the category where it belongs. Alphabetize each category.

(Reminder: Authors are alphabetized with their last name first. Example: Marion E. Gridley is listed as Gridley, Marion E.)

A	Gallant, Roy A.
S	Indians
T	Animals of Long Ago
S	gardens
T	The White House
A	Sandak, Cass R.
T	The Pony Express
A	Herbst, Judith
S	pilgrims
T	The Hobbit
A	Dicerto, Joseph J.
S	planets

AUTHOR
Dicerto, Joseph J.
Gallant, Roy A.
Herbst, Judith
Sandak, Cass R.

Title
Animals of Long Ago
The Hobbit
The Pony Express
The White House

Subject
Gardens
Indians
Pilgrims
Planets

36

Library Skills

Directions: Look at the number on each book. Then use the Dewey Decimal System directory to find out what the book is about. Write the subject of the book on the line.

All libraries that use the Dewey Decimal System follow the same order. For example, all books between 500-599 have to do with science. All books between 900-999 have to do with history. Each library divides its system even further. For example, one library may have kites at 796.15, while another library may have kites at 791.13.

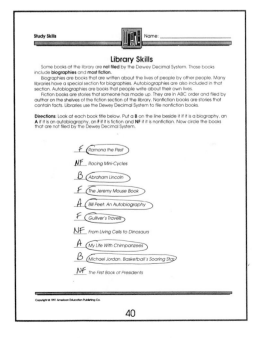

560 — *Fossils*   915.2 — *Japan*   391 — *Costumes*   612 — *Human Body*   599 — *Bigfoot*

793.8 — *Magic*   796.4 — *Gymnastics*   923.1 — *Presidents*   636.9 — *Pets*   581 — *Planets*

Dewey Decimal System directory

390-399 Costumes	630-639 Pets
560-569 Fossils	790-795 Magic
580-589 Plants	796-799 Gymnastics
595-599 Big Foot	910-919 Japan
610-619 Human Body	920-929 Presidents

39

Library Skills

Look at the three cards from a library card catalog. Each has the same "call number" that shows where to find the book on the library shelves. The other information on the cards is presented differently.

Directions: Answer the questions about what is shown on these cards.

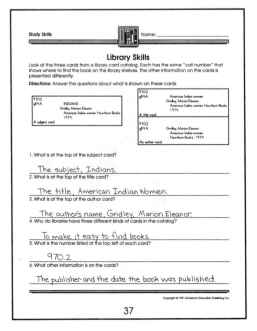

```
970.2
g89A        INDIANS
            Gridley, Marion Eleanor
            American Indian women. Hawthorn Books
            1979
A subject card
```

```
970.2
g89A        American Indian women.
            Gridley, Marion Eleanor
            American Indian women. Hawthorn Books
            1979
A title card
```

```
970.2
g89A        Gridley, Marion Eleanor
            American Indian women.
            Hawthorn Books. 1979
An author card
```

1. What is at the top of the subject card?

   The subject, Indians.

2. What is at the top of the title card?

   The title, American Indian Women.

3. What is at the top of the author card?

   The author's name, Gridley, Marion Eleanor.

4. Why do libraries have three different kinds of cards in the catalog?

   To make it easy to find books.

5. What is the number listed at the top left of each card?

   970.2

6. What other information is on the cards?

   The publisher and the date the book was published.

37

Library Skills

Some books at the library are **not filed** by the Dewey Decimal System. Those books include **biographies** and **most fiction**.

Biographies are books that are written about the lives of people by other people. Many libraries have a special section for biographies. Autobiographies are also included in that section. Autobiographies are books that people write about their own lives.

Fiction books are stories that someone has made up. They are in ABC order and filed by author on the shelves of the fiction section of the library. Nonfiction books are stories that contain facts. Libraries use the Dewey Decimal System to file nonfiction books.

Directions: Look at each book title below. Put a **B** on the line beside it if it is a biography, an **A** if it is an autobiography, an **F** if it is fiction and **NF** if it is nonfiction. Now circle the books that are not filed by the Dewey Decimal System.

F	(Ramona the Pest)
NF	Racing Mini-Cycles
B	Abraham Lincoln
F	(The Jeremy Mouse Book)
A	(Bill Peet: An Autobiography)
F	(Gulliver's Travels)
NF	From Living Cells to Dinosaurs
A	(My Life With Chimpanzees)
B	(Michael Jordan, Basketball's Soaring Star)
NF	The First Book of Presidents

40

Library Skills

Directions: Now go to the library! Use your new library skills to answer the questions below.

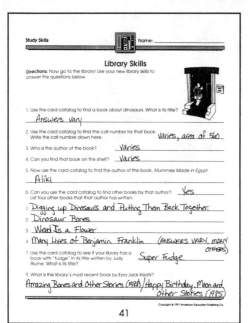

1. Use the card catalog to find a book about dinosaurs. What is its title?
Answers vary

2. Use the card catalog to find the call number for that book. Write the call number down here.   _Varies, area of 560_

3. Who is the author of the book? _Varies_

4. Can you find that book on the shelf? _Varies_

5. Now use the card catalog to find the author of the book, *Mummies Made in Egypt*.
Aliki

6. Can you use the card catalog to find other books by that author? _Yes_
List four other books that that author has written.
1. _Digging up Dinosaurs and Putting Them Back Together._
2. _Dinosaur Bones_
3. _Weed Is a Flower_
4. _Many Lives of Benjamin Franklin_   (ANSWERS VARY, MANY OTHERS)

7. Use the card catalog to see if your library has a book with "fudge" in its title written by Judy Blume. What is its title?   _Super Fudge_

8. What is the library's most recent book by Ezra Jack Keats?
Amazing Bones and Other Stories (1980)/ Happy Birthday, Moon and Other Stories (1985)

41

Introducing Library Skills

Before you to look up something in an encyclopedia, think about the best word to use for it. For example, if you really want to know about ducks, look up the word duck. But if you're interested in knowing something about mallard ducks, then look up mallard ducks in the encyclopedia's index. The index shows the page number and book number, or volume, where the information is located.

Look at the index entry below about Neil Armstrong. Most index entries also tell you when a person lived and died. They will also give you a short description of who the person is.

> **ARMSTRONG, NEIL**   United States astronaut, b. 1930,
> was commander of Gemini 8 1966, was the first man to
> walk on the Moon, July 1969.
> references in
>   Astronaut illus 2:56
>   Space travel 17:21%

For example, Neil Armstrong is listed under Astronaut. This entry shows that there is an illustration of Neil Armstrong in 2:56. That means that it is in Volume 2, or the second book in the set of encyclopedias, on page 56. If there is an "a" listed, it means that the article is in the column on the left. If there is a "b" listed, it means it is in the column on the right.

If Neil Armstrong were listed as an article in the encyclopedia, the index would tell you that. It would say something like:

> main article Armstrong, Neil
> 2:87

Directions: Answer the questions about using the encyclopedia's index.

1. According to the index listing for Neil Armstrong, when was he born? _1930_

   Has he died yet? _No_

2. Use the index listing to tell who Neil Armstrong was. _First man to walk on the Moon_

3. Use the listing to find out when he walked on the moon. _July, 1969_

4. Where does this index say you can find information about Neil Armstrong?
Under astronaut or space travel.

44

Review

Directions: Follow the instructions for each set of questions.

1. Write **A, S** or **T** beside each line below to say if you would look under author, subject or title in the card catalog at the library.
- _S_ dinosaurs
- _S_ Russia
- _A_ Scarry, Richard
- _A_ Christopher, Matt
- _A_ Milne, A.A.
- _T_ *The Arctic and the Antarctic*
- _T_ *The Figure in the Shadows*
- _S_ Eskimos

2. Write **True** or **False** beside each sentence.
- _F_ A biography is a story that someone writes about him or herself.
- _F_ Fiction is a book that uses facts.
- _T_ Fiction is a book that some one made up.
- _T_ Nonfiction uses facts.
- _T_ An autobiography is a story that someone writes about him or herself.
- _T_ A biography is the story of someone's life.

3. Look at the library card. Identify the parts that are numbered.

> 560 ¹
> DINOSAURS ²
> Shapp, Martha and Charles. ³
> Animals of long ago. ⁴ Franklin Watts. ⁶
> 1968. ⁵

1. _Call number_
2. _Subject_
3. _Authors_
4. _Title_
5. _Date it was published_
6. _Publisher_

42

Using The Encyclopedia

Directions: Answer each question about using the encyclopedia.

1. You want to find information about the Tyrannosaurus (Ty-ran-o-sor-us) Rex dinosaur. What would you do first?
Look in the encyclopedia index.

2. If there is no listing in the index for Tyrannosaurus, what other subject would you look under?
Dinosaurs

3. You want to find information about President George Bush. Under which index entry would you look?
Bush, George.

4. If there is no separate entry for George Bush, where else could you look?
Under "President."

5. Why should you use the encyclopedia index first?
It tells you exactly where to find the information.

6. If the encyclopedia says that Tyrannosaurus is in 17:97, what does that mean?
It is in the 17ᵗʰ volume on page 97.

7. If the encyclopedia says "references in," does that refer you to a main article about the subject?
_No_

8. Is there always only one place to find a subject in the encyclopedia? Why or why not?
No, there can be many places a subject is mentioned.

9. Will an encyclopedia index tell you when a person was born? _Yes_

10. You want to find information about the Discovery Spaceship. How would you find it.
First look in the index under Discovery. If it is not there, look under Spaceship.

45

Introducing Encyclopedia Skills

Encyclopedias are sets of books that give information about different subjects. For example, if you want to know when cars were first made, an encyclopedia could tell you.

Encyclopedias come in sets of 20 or 30 books. They contain a lot of facts. They are called reference books. Each subject listed in them is called an entry.

Some of the best encyclopedias for children are *World Book Encyclopedia, Compton's Encyclopedia* or *Children's Britannica*. Some encyclopedias are built around only one subject. *The McGraw-Hill Encyclopedia of Science and Technology* is one of those encyclopedias.

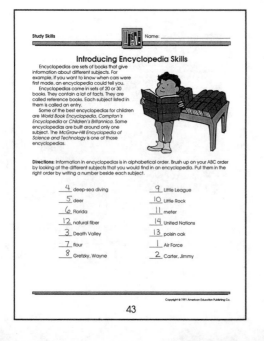

Directions: Information in encyclopedias is in alphabetical order. Brush up on your ABC order by looking at the different subjects that you would find in an encyclopedia. Put them in the right order by writing a number beside each subject.

- _4_ deep-sea diving
- _5_ deer
- _6_ Florida
- _12_ natural fiber
- _3_ Death Valley
- _7_ flour
- _8_ Gretzky, Wayne
- _9_ Little League
- _10_ Little Rock
- _11_ meter
- _14_ United Nations
- _13_ poisin oak
- _1_ Air Force
- _2_ Carter, Jimmy

43

Introducing Encyclopedia Skills

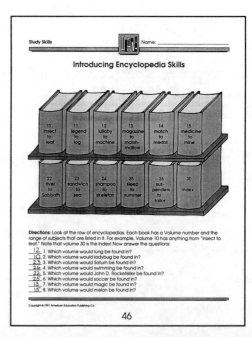

Directions: Look at the row of encyclopedias. Each book has a Volume number and the range of subjects that are listed in it. For example, Volume 10 has anything from "insect to leaf." Note that volume 30 is the Index! Now answer the questions:

- _12_ 1. Which volume would lung be found in?
- _10_ 2. Which volume would ladybug be found in?
- _23_ 3. Which volume would Saturn be found in?
- _36_ 4. Which volume would swimming be found in?
- _22_ 5. Which volume would John D. Rockefeller be found in?
- _25_ 6. Which volume would soccer be found in?
- _13_ 7. Which volume would magic be found in?
- _15_ 8. Which volume would melon be found in?

46

80

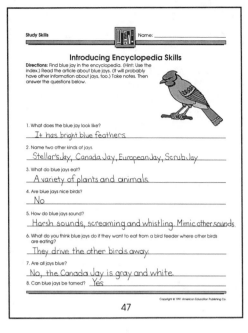 Name: _____

Introducing Encyclopedia Skills

Directions: Find blue jay in the encyclopedia. (Hint: Use the index.) Read the article about blue jays. (It will probably have other information about jays, too.) Take notes. Then answer the questions below.

1. What does the blue jay look like?

It has bright blue feathers.

2. Name two other kinds of jays.

Stellar's Jay, Canada Jay, European Jay, Scrub Jay

3. What do blue jays eat?

A variety of plants and animals.

4. Are blue jays nice birds?

No

5. How do blue jays sound?

Harsh sounds, screaming and whistling. Mimic other sounds.

6. What do you think blue jays do if they want to eat from a bird feeder where other birds are eating?

They drive the other birds away.

7. Are all jays blue?

No, the Canada Jay is gray and white.

8. Can blue jays be tamed? Yes

47

 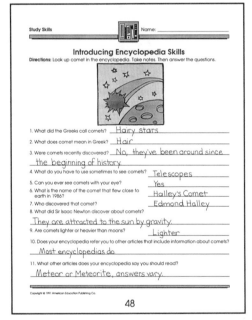 Name: _____

Introducing Encyclopedia Skills

Directions: Look up comet in the encyclopedia. Take notes. Then answer the questions.

1. What did the Greeks call comets? Hairy stars

2. What does comet mean in Greek? Hair

3. Were comets recently discovered? No, they've been around since the beginning of history.

4. What do you have to use sometimes to see comets? Telescopes

5. Can you ever see comets with your eye? Yes

6. What is the name of the comet that flew close to earth in 1986? Halley's Comet

7. Who discovered that comet? Edmond Halley

8. What did Sir Isaac Newton discover about comets?

They are attracted to the sun by gravity.

9. Are comets lighter or heavier than moons? Lighter

10. Does your encyclopedia refer you to other articles that include information about comets?

Most encyclopedias do.

11. What other articles does your encyclopedia say you should read?

Meteor or Meteorite, answers vary.

48

 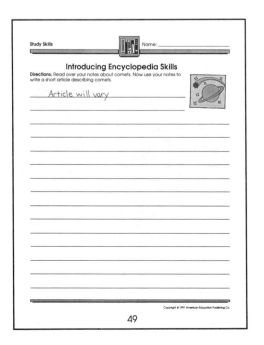 Name: _____

Introducing Encyclopedia Skills

Directions: Read over your notes about comets. Now use your notes to write a short article describing comets.

Article will vary

49

81

 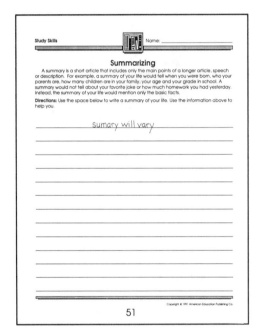 Name: _____

Review

Directions: Look at each question. Follow the instructions.

1. Read each question. Write **True** or **False** on the line beside it.

F Every subject you look up in an encyclopedia will have a whole article written about it.
T You should always use the index to find a subject in the encyclopedia.
T An index may refer you to more than one articles about a subject.
F Entries in an encyclopedia are in order according to when they happened.
T The index will give you some information about your subject.

2. Put the following subjects in ABC order. Write the number of its order on the line beside it.

4 Bush, George
7 meteor
8 planets
2 Brazil
3 bush
10 William I
9 whole wheat flour
6 Lincoln, Abraham
1 Bell, Alexander Graham
5 Japan

3. Name two places where you could look to find Jupiter in an encyclopedia.

Jupiter   Planets   Solar System

4. Name two possible entries for George Washington in an encyclopedia.

Washington, George or Presidents

5. Name one entry that would include information about ants, flies, spiders and gnats.

Insects or Bugs

50

Name: _____

Summarizing

A summary is a short article that includes only the main points of a longer article, speech or description. For example, a summary of your life would tell when you were born, who your parents are, how many children are in your family, your age and your grade in school. A summary would not tell about your favorite joke or how much homework you had yesterday. Instead, the summary of your life would mention only the basic facts.

Directions: Use the space below to write a summary of your life. Use the information above to help you.

sumary will vary

51

Name: _____

The Cold North Pole

At the North Pole the sun does not shine for half of the year. It stays dark outside. But for the other six months of the year the sun does not set. It is light through the night.

The North Pole is as far north as you can go. If you traveled north to the North Pole and kept going, you would start going south. You could call the North Pole the top of the earth.

The average temperature at the north pole is -9 degrees Fahrenheit. That is not much colder than a lot of towns in the United States get in the winter. In fact, some towns get colder than that. But at the North Pole it stays very cold for a very long time.

With the sun out for 24 hours, the North Pole can get as warm as 38 degrees Fahrenheit in the summer. But that is not quite warm enough to swim, is it?

The cold winds that blow off of the Arctic Ocean make the North Pole a very cold place. The summer temperature only gets to 38 degrees in places that are sheltered from the wind.

The Arctic Ocean is at the North Pole. The area surrounding the North Pole is called the Arctic Region. Some of Canada, Alaska, Greenland, Russia and Scandinavia (Skan-di-na-via) are in the Arctic Region. These places get very cold in the long, dark winters, too!

The main points of this story include: 1. The sun is never out in the winter. It is always out in the summer. 2. The North Pole is very cold all year. 3. Winds from the Arctic Ocean make the North Pole stay very cold. 4. The Arctic Ocean surrounds the North Pole. 4. There is some land in the Arctic Region.

Directions: Write a paragraph that summarizes conditions at the North Pole. Use another sheet of paper if necessary.

answer will vary but should be based on the main points listed above.

52

Eskimos: Great Hunters and Fishermen

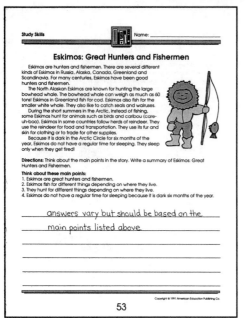

Eskimos are hunters and fishermen. There are several different kinds of Eskimos in Russia, Alaska, Canada, Greenland and Scandinavia. For many centuries, Eskimos have been good hunters and fishermen.

The North Alaskan Eskimos are known for hunting the large bowhead whale. The bowhead whale can weigh as much as 60 tons! Eskimos in Greenland fish for cod. Eskimos also fish for the smaller white whale. They also like to catch seals and walruses.

During the short summers in the Arctic, instead of fishing, some Eskimos hunt for animals such as birds and caribou (care-uh-boo). Eskimos in some countries follow herds of reindeer. They use the reindeer for food and transportation. They use its fur and skin for clothing or to trade for other supplies.

Because it is dark in the Arctic Circle for six months of the year, Eskimos do not have a regular time for sleeping. They sleep only when they get tired!

Directions: Think about the main points in the story. Write a summary of Eskimos: Great Hunters and Fishermen.

Think about these main points:
1. Eskimos are great hunters and fishermen.
2. Eskimos fish for different things depending on where they live.
3. They hunt for different things depending on where they live.
4. Eskimos do not have a regular time for sleeping because it is dark six months of the year.

answers vary but should be based on the
main points listed above

53

Mr. Audubon's Birds

John James Audubon (Aw-do-bon) is well known for his study of birds in the early 1800's. He found studying birds more exciting than any career.

When he was nine years old and living in France, John Audubon was sent to a special school so he could become a sea captain. But he was not a good student. He spent too much time outside watching birds and animals!

When he was 17, his father sent him to America to take care of his large home near Philadelphia. Again, the birds and the wildlife caught his eye.

During all this time, Mr. Audubon painted pictures of birds. He often killed birds so that he could paint pictures of them. Some people say that is what made him different from other artists. He did not paint his pictures from birds that were in museums.

John Audubon loved birds. When Mr. Audubon was 40 years old he sold several life-size pictures of his birds. He became famous!

Mr. Audubon's name is still popular among people who like the outdoors. Today the National Audubon Society, named in his honor, works hard to save birds and wildlife.

Directions: Think about the main points of the story about Mr. Audubon's birds. Write a summary about it.

Here are a couple main points of the story. Can you think of others?
1. Mr. Audubon studied birds in the early 1800s.

2. He didn't do well at other jobs.

3. _He painted pictures of birds._

4. _Mr. Audubon became famous._

5. _The National Audubon Society was formed after he died._

Now summarize the story about Mr. Audubon's Birds.

answer varies

56

Settler Children Were Very Busy

In the 1700s and 1800s many children came to America from other countries. In the beginning, they had no time to go to school. They had to help their families work in the fields, care for the animals and clean the house. They also helped care for their younger brothers and sisters.

Sometimes settler children helped build houses and schools. Usually these early school buildings were just one room. There was only one teacher for all the children. Settler children were very happy when they could attend school.

Because settler children worked so much, they had little time to play. There were not many things settler children could do just for fun. One pastime was gardening. Weeding their gardens taught them how to be orderly. Children sometimes made gifts out of the things they grew.

The settlers also encouraged their children to sing. Each one was expected to play at least one musical instrument. Parents wanted their settler children to walk, ride horses, visit friends and relatives and read nonfiction books.

Most settler children did not have many toys. The toys they owned were made by their parents and grandparents. They were made of cloth or carved from wood. The children made up games out of string, such as "cat's cradle." They also made things out of wood, such as see-saws. Settler children did not have all the toys we have today, but they managed to have fun, anyway!

Directions: What are the main points about the first children who came to the United States? Write a summary about settler children.

Here are two main points of the story. Can you name any others?

1. Settler children worked hard.

2. Settler children had many jobs.

3. _Settler children liked school._

4. _Settler children had little time for playing._

5. _Settler children had few toys._

Summary:

answer varies

54

Summarizing

Directions: Read a story or a short book that you choose from your library. Take notes about its main points. Then use this page to write a summary of the story.

What is the title of your story?

Answers will vary, teachers or
parents should check the child's
notes too.

57

Express Mail

Few of us think of the postal service as an interesting place to work. However, mail carriers of yesteryear led an exciting and sometimes dangerous life.

Before 1860, mail delivery was not organized. It could take a westerner months to receive a letter or newspaper from "back east." When the Civil War broke out, it became important to spread news of the war to all citizens. A 2,000 mile mail route was organized. It began in Missouri and went through Kansas, Nebraska, Colorado, Wyoming, Utah and Nevada.

Using a relay system, men on ponies carried the mail to other riders, who in turn carried it to others, and so on until it reached its destination. The mail delivery system was called Pony Express, and those early mail carriers found their jobs very exciting. They rode their ponies fast and hard, and rarely stopped to rest. Have you ever heard the expression, "The mail must get through?" It sprang up during the year and a half that Pony Express operated. Between April 1860 and October 1891, Pony Express riders covered 616,000 miles on horseback.

By 1861 telegraph wires had been strung across most of the country. Messages about the war — or anything else — could be sent and received quickly over telegraph wires using a system called Morse Code. Morse Code used a series of dots and dashes that stood for letters of the alphabet. The first telegraph message sent from California to President Abraham Lincoln ended the need for the Pony Express.

Directions: Think about the main points in the story about the Pony Express. Then write a summary about it. Use another sheet of paper if you need to.

Here are a couple main points of this story. Can you name others?

1. Mail delivery used to be exciting.

2. Pony Express started in 1860 because of the Civil War.

3. _News was hard to get west of Missouri_

4. _Pony Express riders raced from one state to the next._

5. _Pony Express ended in 1861 when telegraph lines were finished._

Summary:

answer varies

55

Review

Finding the American Dream

Mary McLeod Bethune was born into a poor black family. Today there is a memorial in Washington, D.C., that honors her. She found the American Dream because she lived a successful life!

Mary Jane McLeod's parents were slaves in South Carolina. She had 16 brothers and sisters. Mary Jane was born right after her parents were freed from slavery. She was also the first in her family to get an education.

After she finished school, Mary Jane received an invitation to study at a black girls' school in North Carolina. After spending seven years at that school, she tried to travel to Africa to teach the people there. She could not get the support from the people that she needed, so she taught school in Chicago instead.

In 1904 Mary McLeod Bethune opened a school for black girls in Daytona Beach, Florida. That school became a college, the Bethune-Cookman College that is still in Daytona Beach. In 1974 the Mary McLeod Bethune Memorial was built in Washington, D.C. Mary McLeod Bethune certainly lived the American Dream!

Directions: Think about the above story's main points. Then write a summary about it.

The main points in this story are:

1. Mary McLeod Bethune lived the American Dream.

2. _Her parents were slaves._

3. _Mary McLeod went to a black girls school in North Carolina._

4. _She opened a school in Daytona Beach in 1984._

5. _The Mary McLeod Bethune memorial was built in Washington, D.C._

Summary:

answer varies

58

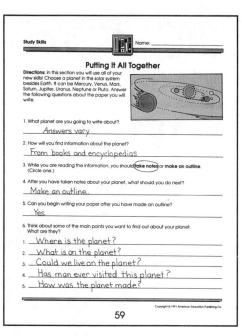 Name: _____

Putting It All Together

Directions: In this section you will use all of your new skills! Choose a planet in the solar system besides Earth. It can be Mercury, Venus, Mars, Saturn, Jupiter, Uranus, Neptune or Pluto. Answer the following questions about the paper you will write.

1. What planet are you going to write about?
   _____ Answers vary _____

2. How will you find information about the planet?
   From books and encyclopedias

3. While you are reading the information, you should (take notes) or **make an outline.** (Circle one.)

4. After you have taken notes about your planet, what should you do next?
   Make an outline.

5. Can you begin writing your paper after you have made an outline?
   Yes

6. Think about some of the main points you want to find out about your planet. What are they?
   1. Where is the planet?
   2. What is on the planet?
   3. Could we live on the planet?
   4. Has man ever visited this planet?
   5. How was the planet made?

59

Name: _____

Putting It All Together

Directions: It is time to make an outline for your paper about the planet. Look at the outline below. Some of the main points have already been filled in. Complete your outline using the information you have found in books and the encyclopedia.

I. The location of the planet
  A. How far?
    1. From Earth
    2. From the Sun
  B. What are its neighbors?

II. What does the planet look like?
  A. Is it a special color?
  B. How many moons does it have?

III. What is on the planet?
  A. Are there plants?
  B. Is there dust?
  C. Is there wind?

IV. Could we live here? Why or why not?
  A. Is there any air?
  B. Is there any water?
  C. Is there any gravity?

62

Name: _____

Putting It All Together

Directions: Look at each question about your planet. Follow the instructions.

1. To begin gathering information about your planet you should look for books about it. Besides books with the planet's name in the title, what other books may have facts about the planet?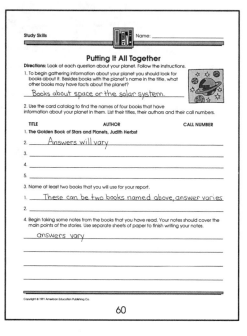
   Books about space or the solar system.

2. Use the card catalog to find the names of four books that have information about your planet in them. List their titles, their authors and their call numbers.

TITLE	AUTHOR	CALL NUMBER
1. The Golden Book of Stars and Planets, Judith Herbst		
2. Answers will vary		
3.		
4.		
5.		

3. Name at least two books that you will use for your report.
   1. These can be two books named above, answer varies
   2.

4. Begin taking some notes from the books that you have read. Your notes should cover the main points of the stories. Use separate sheets of paper to finish writing your notes.
   answers vary

60

Name: _____

Putting It All Together

Directions: Now use your outline and your notes to begin writing a paper about the planet. Use your own paper to finish this writing project.

_____ Answers, papers will vary _____

63

 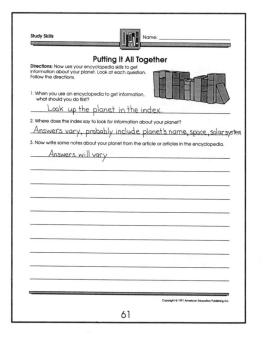 Name: _____

Putting It All Together

Directions: Now use your encyclopedia skills to get information about your planet. Look at each question. Follow the directions.

1. When you use an encyclopedia to get information, what should you do first?
   Look up the planet in the index.

2. Where does the index say to look for information about your planet?
   Answers vary, probably include planet's name, space, solar system

3. Now write some notes about your planet from the article or articles in the encyclopedia.
   Answers will vary

61

83

Name: _____

Review

Directions: Read each question. Follow the instructions.

1. Write **True** or **False** beside each statement.
   F Card catalogs have four different files.
   T You can find a book if all you know is the author's name.
   T Call numbers are listed in the card catalog.
   F All books in a library are filed by their call numbers.
   T Biographies have their own section in some libraries.
   T When you take notes you must write in complete sentences.
   F Never abbreviate when you take notes.
   F You should write down a lot when you take notes.
   T Before you take notes, you should ask yourself what you would like to know.

2. Write the form for an outline.
   I. Main Idea
     A. A smaller idea
     B. Another smaller idea.
       1. Example.
       2. Example.
   II. Second main idea.
     A. A smaller idea.
     B. Another smaller idea.
       1. Example.
   III. Third main idea.

3. What do you do when you summarize a story?
   You put all the main ideas together in a short form.

64

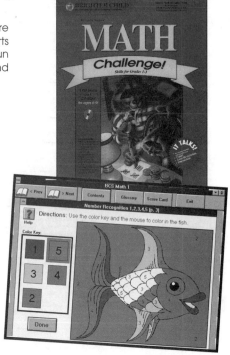

84

OVERVIEW

ENRICHMENT READING is designed to provide children with practice in reading and to increase students' reading abilities. The program consists of six editions, one each for grades 1 through 6. The major areas of reading instruction--word skills, vocabulary, study skills, comprehension, and literary forms--are covered as appropriate at each level.

ENRICHMENT READING provides a wide range of activities that target a variety of skills in each instructional area. The program is unique because it helps children expand their skills in playful ways with games, puzzles, riddles, contests, and stories. The high-interest activities are informative and fun to do.

Home involvement is important to any child's success in school. *ENRICHMENT READING* is the ideal vehicle for fostering home involvement. Every lesson provides specific opportunities for children to work with a parent, a family member, an adult, or a friend.

AUTHORS

Peggy Kaye, the author of *ENRICHMENT READING*, is also an author of *ENRICHMENT MATH* and the author of two parent/teacher resource books, *Games for Reading* and *Games for Math.* Currently, Ms. Kaye divides her time between writing books and tutoring students in reading and math. She has also taught for ten years in New York City public and private schools.

WRITERS

Timothy J. Baehr is a writer and editor of instructional materials on the elementary, secondary, and college levels. Mr. Baehr has also authored an award-winning column on bicycling and a resource book for writers of educational materials.

Cynthia Benjamin is a writer of reading instructional materials, television scripts, and original stories. Ms. Benjamin has also tutored students in reading at the New York University Reading Institute.

Russell Ginns is a writer and editor of materials for a children's science and nature magazine. Mr. Ginn's speciality is interactive materials, including games, puzzles, and quizzes.

WHY ENRICHMENT READING?

Enrichment and parental involvement are both crucial to children's success in school, and educators recognize the important role work done at home plays in the educational process. Enrichment activities give children opportunities to practice, apply, and expand their reading skills, while encouraging them to think while they read. *ENRICHMENT READING* offers exactly this kind of opportunity. Each lesson focuses on an important reading skill and involves children in active learning. Each lesson will entertain and delight children.

When childen enjoy their lessons and are involved in the activities, they are naturally alert and receptive to learning. They understand more. They remember more. All children enjoy playing games, having contests, and solving puzzles. They like reading interesting stories, amusing stories, jokes, and riddles. Activities such as these get children involved in reading. This is why these kinds of activities form the core of *ENRICHMENT READING.*

Each lesson consists of two parts. Children complete the first part by themselves. The second part is completed together with a family member, an adult, or a friend. *ENRICHMENT READING* activities do not require people at home to teach reading. Instead, the activities involve everyone in enjoyable reading games and interesting language experiences.

Page 65   1. Lightning Lobby 2. Dead End 3. Spider Den 4. east 5. north 6. Mummy Parlor 7. Evil Entry

Page 66   *Crossed-out sentences:* Stephanie's older sister was also an actress. Once Bobby played on a park bench through a rainstorm. Reid also likes to surf and water ski. Her father sold airplanes and there was an airfield behind her house.; young people who have done unusual or interesting things

Page 67   1. Schoolhouse 2. Mr. and Mrs. Bridges 3. Gold Mine, Jail 4. herb jars, flour sack 5. outlaws 6. Gold Mine 7. Miss Hastings; answers will vary

Page 68   Results and answers will vary.

Page 69   *The Record:* hurricane near Florida *The Gazette:* sudden winter storm *The Sun:* escaped farm animals *The News:* movie star disappeared *The Advance:* scientists using powerful new telescopes; reasons will vary

Page 70   cowboy

Page 71   1. e 2. n. 3. g 4. i 5. n 6. e 7. e 8. r 9. s; engineers

Page 72   Answers will vary.